paddling with the current

Pierre Elliott Trudeau, Étienne Parent,
liberalism, and nationalism in Canada

CLAUDE COUTURE

paddling
with the
current

Pierre Elliott Trudeau,
Étienne Parent,
liberalism,
and nationalism
in Canada

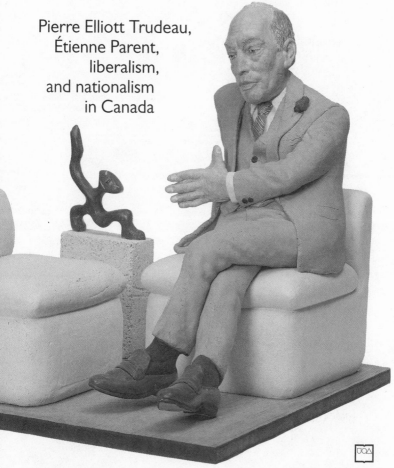

Translated from
French by Vivien Bosley

The University
of Alberta Press

ISBN 0–88864–313–6
This edition published by
   The University of Alberta Press
   141 Athabasca Hall
   Edmonton, Alberta, Canada T6G 2E8

F
1034.3
.T7
C5713
1998

Original French-language edition copyright © Harmattan inc., 1996
English-language edition copyright © The University of Alberta Press, 1998

Originally published as *La loyauté d'un laïc: Pierre Elliott Trudeau et le libéralisme canadien*
by Harmattan inc., Paris and Montréal, 1996.

Canadian Cataloguing in Publication Data

Couture, Claude, 1955–
   Paddling with the current

   Translation of: La loyauté d'un laïc.
   Includes bibliographical references.
   ISBN 0–88864–313–6

   1. Trudeau, Pierre Elliott, 1919- —Views on liberalism. 2. Liberalism—Canada. 3.
Nationalism—Quebec (Province) 4. Nationalism—Canada. I. Title.
FC626.T7C6813 1998   320.51′0971   C98-910365–X
F1034.3.T7C6813 1998

∞ Printed on acid-free paper.
Printed and bound in Canada by Hignell Book Printing Ltd., Winnipeg, Manitoba.

The University of Alberta Press acknowledges the financial support of the Government of
Canada through the Book Publishing Industry Development Program for its publishing
activities. The Press also gratefully acknowledges the support received for its program from
the Canada Council for the Arts and the Alberta Foundation for the Arts.

Cover image: Joe Fafard, "Pierre," 1984. Earthenware, acrylic, porous brick, plywood.
Collection of the Mendel Art Gallery. Purchased with funds from the Canada Council
Special Purchase Assistance Program and monies raised by the Gallery Group 1984. Photo by
Grant Kernan, A.K. Photos, Saskatoon. Used by permission of the artist.

ALBERTA Lotteries

The Alberta Foundation for the Arts

Alberta COMMUNITY DEVELOPMENT

COMMITTED TO THE DEVELOPMENT OF CULTURE AND THE ARTS

THE CANADA COUNCIL FOR THE ARTS SINCE 1957 | LE CONSEIL DES ARTS DU CANADA DEPUIS 1957

To Yasmeen

contents

acknowledgements

MANY COLLEAGUES HAVE PATIENTLY READ this manuscript. Their support and critical comments were very important. I would like to thank particularly Dr. Yasmeen Abu-Laban and Dr. Allan Tupper from the Department of Political Science at the University of Alberta; Dr. Claude Denis and Dr. Donald Ipperciel from the Faculté Saint–Jean at the University of Alberta; Dr. Ian Angus from Simon Fraser University and Dr. Kenneth McRoberts from York University; and Dr. Linda Cardinal and Dr. Gilles Paquet from the University of Ottawa.

The research for this project was financed by the Small Faculties Research Programme of the University of Alberta and by the Institut de recherche de la Faculté Saint–Jean at the University of Alberta. Special thanks to the students who contributed to the research: Dianne Killips, Paul Bourassa, Denis Perreaux, and Josée Thibeault.

This project would never have materialized without the help, encouragement, and vision of Glenn Rollans, Director of the University of Alberta Press, and Leslie Vermeer, the project editor. And finally, I would like to thank translator Vivien

Bosley, Professor of Romance Languages at the University of Alberta, for her excellent work on the text.

introduction

"**T**RUDEAU HAS ALWAYS SEEMED to be a gentlemanly kind of person. I distrust his distrust of traditional French Canada and I fear his naivety about the nature of English-speaking society."
—*George Grant to Hugh MacLennan, 27 March 1969.*

In the first issue of the journal *Cité libre* in 1950, Pierre Elliott Trudeau wrote, "What French Canada needs is a positive philosophy of action."[1] He continued,

> For in fact, we have contributed nothing to the society of mankind. We've survived, so to speak, by eating up the abundant capital of raw materials bequeathed to us by nature, and by exhausting the rich human potential France was kind enough to give us.[2]

The rest is well known—in Canada, at least. *Cité libre* became the headquarters of the opponents of the rule of the provincial premier, Maurice Lenoblet Duplessis. Pierre Elliott Trudeau was the acknowledged intellectual leader of this opposition.

The 1960s were the turning-point when a coalition of liberals and progressives, in conjunction with workers' trades unions, took over provincial power in Quebec and began a series of reforms unimaginable hitherto. The Quiet Revolution was underway.

Although he had certainly played a key role in laying the ground for the Quiet Revolution, which was such a rupturing event for many people, Pierre Elliott Trudeau remained on the fringe of active politics and of federal and provincial power structures until 1965. In September of that year, however, along with the journalist Gérard Pelletier and trade union leader Jean Marchand, Trudeau announced he would run as candidate for the federal Liberal Party in the election on 8 November 1965. Once elected, the three friends (nicknamed the Three Wise Men), became ministers in the Lester Pearson government. In 1968, Pierre Elliott Trudeau succeeded Lester Pearson as head of the Liberal Party of Canada, and in April 1968, became Prime Minister of the country. On 25 June 1968, the Liberal party of Canada won 155 of the 264 seats in the House of Commons and formed a majority government, the first after six years of minority governments.

From the moment of his election, and throughout the next sixteen years, Pierre Elliott Trudeau dominated Canadian politics, and, in one way or another, has continued to wield an extraordinary influence, even after his retirement from political life in 1984. Right up to the present day, through his pronouncements and publications (particularly *Memoirs* in 1993 and the republication of various writings as *Against the Current* in 1996), Pierre Elliott Trudeau continues both to fascinate us and to provoke highly emotional reactions—especially among English Canadians, but also among Quebeckers, despite their pretense of indifference.

Through his well-timed and effective intervention, Pierre Elliott Trudeau was largely responsible for the failure of the Meech Lake (1990) and Charlottetown (1992) accords on the Constitution. At least Trudeau's statements offered a justification for an opposition to these accords based on a vision of federalism different from the principles of both Meech and Charlottetown. Thus the institutions of the Trudeau era remained intact. The 1995 Quebec referendum, however, which the federalists won by the narrowest margin imaginable, showed to what extent Canada—far from having resolved its national questions in general, and the Quebec question in particular—remains unstable. Hence the following paradox: since the 1960s, under the political and intellectual leadership of the man who was, according to many contemporaries, the most charismatic Canadian leader of the twentieth century, the Canadian state seems ever more precarious and ever more undermined by a crisis of credibility. Furthermore, whereas Pierre Elliott Trudeau was a tireless opponent of strict nationalism and collective rights, the last decades have been marked by an unquestionable rise of nationalisms: Quebec nationalism, aboriginal nationalism, and even "Canadian" nationalism, the last one characterized by a denial of itself or a denial (sometimes only symbolic) of recognition of other collectivities within Canadian society. How are these paradoxes to be explained?

One possible explanation can be sought in the contradictions in the thought of Trudeau himself. Both as intellectual and politician, Trudeau made, ironically, a vast contribution to the birth of contemporary Quebec nationalism. On the intellectual level, Trudeau, considered by others and by himself to be a liberal thinker, seems unwittingly to have imposed collectivist, determinist, and anti-individualist concepts. In the process—and in spite of a few slight variations in his texts—he was one of the intellectuals of the fifties who created the image of a monolithic French-Canadian society. On the political level, what Trudeau actually did was to use an abstract, metaphysical definition of individual rights to reproduce, apparently without critical reflection, one of the key elements of Anglo-American culture: in this case, the idea that English and American liberty is superior to the concept of liberty in other cultures. In constructing a nation, as Trudeau attempted to do, on the basis of the principle of individual rights mainly confined to one culture, the former editor of *Cité libre*, despite his own complaints about the Anglo-American pretension of a cultural and moral superiority, managed only to reproduce it and consequently accentuate a form of "Canadian" nationalism. He thus brought about, bizarrely, the hardening of other nationalisms: Quebec and aboriginal.

The first two chapters of this book are devoted to showing the mechanisms and contradictions of Trudeauist thought from his writings in the 1950s. The fourth chapter gives specific examples, from his years in power, of Trudeau's reproduction of some of the ambiguities that already governed his vision of French Canada in the 1950s. From this it will be possible to discern the place Trudeau occupied in Canadian politics—not such a startling position, perhaps, since Trudeau himself, while claiming to be a champion of individualism, contributed to the creation of a collectivist image of French Canada that had been profoundly influenced by the Anglo-American view of itself and other societies. Far from going "against the current"—and contrary to the title of this latest edition of Trudeau's writings (1996)— Trudeauism appears to be a doctrine inherited from Anglo-American historicist thought, which, despite its individualist claims, can be, as we will demonstrate, strongly tainted with collectivism and nationalism.[3] Hence the fundamental misunderstandings in Canadian politics since the 1960s. The man who lashed out at the "new betrayal of the intellectuals," taking as his model the ideas of a daring but similarly contradictory thinker, Julien Benda, ended up repeating the grossest prejudices about the non Anglo-American world current in certain parts of English Canadian society—in particular the idea that French Canada was an ideologically monolithic society until the Quiet Revolution.

In *Orientalism* (1978), Edward Said claims that the essence of colonialism resides in the intellectual representation of the colonized society by the colonizer. So Trudeau, apparently without critical reflection, accepted prejudices about French Canada, held in a most banal way to the view of the forcible colonizer vis-à-vis, in this case, a rival that had come from a colonizing European society but was conquered in 1760. Most of the instability in Canadian politics during the last two decades is rooted in this phenomenon.

In the third chapter, we will see how another intellectual, Étienne Parent, a thinker who is underestimated today but who was strongly influential in the nineteenth century, could have formulated a French Canada without shutting it out of the political and economic liberal sphere. The example of Étienne Parent is important to understanding the fact that French Canada was not the monolithic society described by Trudeau in his early writings.

CHAPTER 1
the asbestos strike

FROM 1950 AND INTO THE SIXTIES, Pierre Elliott Trudeau contributed to the intellectual and political life of Quebec through his frequent articles in the periodical *Cité libre*. In this first section, we will attempt to extrapolate from his writings his basic vision of French Canada. Before dealing with the two specific texts published in *Cité libre*, "Towards a functional policy" and "The new betrayal of the intellectuals," however, we should look at what was certainly the most important and best known of Pierre Elliott Trudeau's texts, the famous first chapter of *The Asbestos Strike*.

FRENCH CANADA AFTER THE SECOND WORLD WAR

In 1956, a group of intellectuals led by Pierre Elliott Trudeau[1] published with Éditions du Jour an analysis of the events surrounding a strike by asbestos industry workers which took place in 1949, mainly in the town of Asbestos. The title of Trudeau's chapter is "The Province of Quebec at the time of the strike." The chapter is divided into three main sections: the "facts," the "ideas," and the "institutions." Let's begin by looking at the "facts."

1

The facts

Trudeau begins by remarking that the number of people in Quebec living in cities increased from forty percent in 1901 to forty-eight percent in 1911, to fifty-six percent in 1921, and to sixty-three percent in 1931. In 1941, the urban population of Quebec stood at sixty-three percent.[2]

In addition, in 1949, at the time of the asbestos strike, primary industries employed only twenty-six percent of the Canadian work-force.[3] In fact, according to Trudeau, "the transformation of the Canadian economy under the impetus of the industrial revolution, corresponded primarily to the profound changes that took place in the two central provinces of Quebec and Ontario: at the turn of the century, they produced between them four–fifths of the total net value of Canadian manufactured goods"; nonetheless, he emphasizes the fact that "in this totality, Quebec played only a secondary role."[4] Workers in Quebec and Ontario represented sixty-one percent of all Canadian workers. They received only sixty-eight percent of wages and salaries; "but Quebec workers' wages were in a proportion of 3.1/5 to that of Ontario workers in 1926, and 3.15/5 in 1949."[5] In other words, Quebec "lagged behind" Ontario, "its development depending on a docile and plentiful workforce rather than on an average of high capital businesses."[6]

He goes on:

We should add ... that Quebec's inferiority in relation to Ontario naturally extends to all sectors of the economy: thus between 1901 and 1948, the hourly wage of a typographer went from $0.24 to $1.52 in Montreal and from $0.26 to $1.78 in Toronto; that of a tramcar driver from $0.16 to $1.00 in Montreal and from $0.18 to $1.10 in Toronto; and that of a brick-layer from $0.30 to $1.60 in Montreal and from $0.37 to $1.75 in Toronto.[7]

And he gives a final example:

> ...from 1939 to 1950, in the manufacturing industry alone, employment rose by 77% and the value of the product (in raw dollars) rose by 93% in Quebec, whereas the percentages for Ontario were 78% and 89%, and for the whole of Canada ... they were 79% and 92%.[8]

In contrast, "the per capita income increased in actual value by 48% in Quebec, by 47% in Ontario and by 54% in the country as a whole."[9]

In short, although the province of Quebec in the first half of the twentieth century had undoubtedly been transformed by the effects of industrialization, at the time of the events of 1949, it "lagged behind" Ontario, according to the editor of *Cité libre*. How is this "lagging behind" to be explained? And based on this assertion, what conclusion could be drawn about the essential nature of French Canadian society? According to Pierre Elliott Trudeau, the answers to these questions lay in the realm of ideas: in the way Canadians pictured the world and themselves at the time of the social and economic transformation brought about by urbanization and industrialization.

The ideas

In the direct style that was already his hallmark, Trudeau offered a trenchant diagnosis of French Canada:

> But in Quebec throughout the first half of the 20th century, our ideas about society were so idealistic, so a priori, so

remote from the facts, in other words so futile, that they never managed to become integrated into dynamic, living institutions. Some of the elements of these ideas should be analyzed, so that the reader can understand how ill-prepared people were at the time of the asbestos strike, to acknowledge, to interpret and to influence the reality of this highly industrialized province which I described above.[10]

He continues,

If my analysis pays little attention to the few centers of liberal free thought which exist on the fringes of what I describe as our ideological monolithism, it is not because I deny their existence ... but rather that an entire people has been persuaded to live on a particular level, whereas all its intellectual and moral disciplines urged it to live on another.[11]

Trudeau says further, "...nationalism was—until the end of the period studied in this book—the main axis around which almost all French-Canadian social thought gravitated."[12] This nationalism is seen to be wholly negative, defined in reaction to

a Protestant, democratic, nationalist, commercial and later on industrial English atmosphere; our nationalism countered this with a defense made up of opposing forces: the French language, Catholicism, authoritarianism, idealism, rural life and later on, a return to the land.[13]

He says, "In the heart of a materialist civilization and in defiance of often shameless politicians, the nationalist school was almost the only one to formulate a thought."[14]

The quotations are eloquent and the thesis clear: in spite of intensive twentieth-century industrialization and urbanization, French-Canadian social thought was bogged down in a nationalist traditionalism completely at odds with the material realities and even the actions of the people. Some passages even take on a Marxist tone when the author describes a "superstructure in which *all* social ideas would be integrated in a homogeneous and logical way."[15] The rest of this section describes the articulation of twentieth-century nationalist thought around an interpretation skewed, according to Trudeau, by the social doctrine of the Church. We'll come back to this. For the time being, we should summarize the state of French-Canadian institutions in the mid-twentieth century according to Pierre Elliott Trudeau.

The institutions

Right at the outset, there was no doubt in Trudeau's mind about the heavy reality of the institutions of French Canada. "Our institutions have created a yawning gap between reality, which is that people were rushing headlong and heedlessly into an industrial era, and theory, which was formulated by doctrinaire thinkers implacably opposed to reality."[16]

Which institutions were these? The most important were la Société Saint Jean–Baptiste (formed in 1834 by Ludger Duvernay), l'École sociale populaire (formed in 1911), and l'Action nationale (formed in 1933); teaching institutions, political parties, and capital and labour represented by business and union organizations.

What were the characteristics of the ideologies turned out by these institutions? According to Trudeau:

Our ideologies, all inspired by distrust of industrialization, by self-reflection, by nostalgia for rural life, no longer corresponded to our ethos, which was unsettled by anonymous capital, preyed upon by foreign influences, and dumped without possessions into a modern junk room where family, neighbors, parish—traditional bulwarks against collapse—no longer offered the same support.[17]

The 1949 strike was a turning point, because it marked the revolt of a people living absolutely in its own time against out-of-date institutions and "rotting" social thought.

There had, of course, been other strikes in French Canada before the asbestos strike, and there would be others after it. But this particular strike was significant because it took place at the end of an age, at exactly the moment when our social framework—in decay because it had been built for a different period—was at the breaking point.[18]

THE THEORY OF THE "FOLK SOCIETY"

This image of a French-Canadian society characterized by a rift between ideology and the "real" world had been commonplace among social scientists and historians since at least the 1930s. To a certain degree, the image had been created initially by American sociologists associated with the "Chicago School," who came to French Canada in the 1930s in search of a "folk society." Trudeau's theory of the rift between social thought and socio-economic reality echoed their work. Two of these authors, Horace Miner (1934) and Everett Hughes (1943), basing their studies on Radcliffe–Brown's structural functionalism and Robert Parks' problematics of urban ecology (Couture and Denis, 1994), used a synchronic approach in their study of examples of French-Canadian communities (Saint–Denis de Kamouraska for Miner and Cantonville–Drummondville for Hughes) that satisfied the criteria of a traditional society. But neither Miner nor Hughes claimed to describe the whole of a society that was already urbanized and industrialized in the 1930s (Handler, 1986).

In 1947, Robert Redfield, who had been Miner's thesis supervisor, defined a traditional society as a small, isolated, illiterate, demographically stable community, that lacked a developed market and in which religious influence outweighed secular. Redfield, Miner, and Hughes thought they could identify several of these characteristics in a society overwhelmed by the phenomena of urbanization and industrialization, but in which there still remained a trace of traditionalism. After the Second World War, however, several Quebec sociologists— among them Marcel Rioux, Jean–Charles Falardeau, and Hubert Guindon—deduced, as did Pierre Elliott Trudeau, that the whole of French Canada was stuck in this outdated ideology. Here, the élite who controlled French-Canadian institutions was generating a nationalist and collectivist discourse based on the values of a so-called traditionalist society. The theory of ideological monolithism was born, giving rise to various methodological, theoretical, and political problems that have not been solved to this day. Let us examine some of these problems.

FRENCH CANADIAN NATIONALISM
AND IDEOLOGICAL MONOLITHISM

How, Trudeau wondered "have we survived" in the face of the out-of-date social-nationalist thought and the incompetence of the élite? He wrote,

In point of fact, by taking no notice of any ideology. Paradoxically, our ethnic group which felt itself honour-bound by its sacred mission and doctrine, owes its survival in no small part, to its "materialism"....

This explains why our people in the half-century preceding the strike never espoused the nationalism of our official thought with its social postulates.[19]

He adds:

Hardly anyone returned to the land or to co-operatism: small business bled to death, co-operatism remained in limbo; and Catholic trades-unionism did not wipe out the other kind. On the contrary, as we saw at the beginning of the chapter, the province underwent a period of intense industrialization, which was remarkably like the kind that was taking place in countries less messianic than ours.[20]

Exactly. At this point in the argument, two questions, of a simply logical nature, arise. If French Canadians have *never* taken any notice of the ideologies of their fossilized élite, how and why did the asbestos strike represent a breaking of the nationalist yoke? In addition, if French Canada was "remarkably like" its neighbors, should we conclude 1) that the people in those "less messianic" countries had never encountered the perverse and impure world of "ideology," or 2) that it was only the French-Canadian élite who was afflicted with the disease of ideology compared to the "less messianic" élite of neighbouring societies? It is true that between 1840 and 1960, English Canada, Great Britain, Germany (after 1871), and France were indeed "less messianic." After all, what does the American conquest of Mexico matter, or their "manifest destiny," the genocide of the aboriginal nations of the Prairies, social Darwinism, racism, especially towards African Americans; what does anti-Semitism, widespread in France, England, Germany, the United States, and English Canada matter; what do the new imperialism of 1880–1914, the two world wars, the cold war matter? All that, supposedly, was less messianic and devoid of ideology.

Another aspect of Pierre Elliott Trudeau's argument, which is in direct contradiction to the idea that nationalism had had no effect, was that the ideological yoke imposed by the French-Canadian élite was an important, if not essential, feature in explaining French Canada's "lagging behind" the rest of the country. What exactly was this "lagging behind"?

To take one example, "in 1926, workers earned 58% of wages paid to all people in Canada. In 1947, this percentage was 61. In Quebec, the percentages had risen from 62 to 66, and in Ontario from 61 to 66."[21] In other words, according to Trudeau himself, the situation in Quebec was identical to that in Ontario. In that case, where was the lag?

Apart from that, let us accept that French-Canadian workers were less well-paid; as a result, the negative impact of traditionalist nationalism should have led to a situation in which the nationalist élites, in their refusal of the modern world, would have sabotaged trade-union organizations in Quebec. But Pierre Elliott Trudeau himself writes that, "in the year of the asbestos strike, 24% of Quebec wage-earners were unionized, a figure slightly above that of Ontario (23%) whereas for the whole of Canada, the proportion was 29%. This figure was increased significantly by British Columbia, with 37% trades union membership."[22] Now in Quebec, in the year of the asbestos strike, Catholic unions formed "35% of the Quebec unionized force."[23] On the basis of these figures, how can one see a fundamental difference between the situation in

Quebec and the reality in the whole of Canada? And how can one not be persuaded of the positive impact of Catholic unionism? There's yet more to come.

Trudeau claims, "Catholic unionism was not the result of altruism, or an attempt to find a cure for the misery of our Catholic, Quebec proletariat. As is the case with a large part of our social doctrine, our unionist ideas sprang from a nationalist reaction against reforms brought in from the outside after our own neglect had failed to apply them in time."[24] Jacques Rouillard (1979) has shown, however, that the Confederation of Catholic Workers of Canada, heirs to the national unions of the beginning of the century (which were themselves heirs to the Chevaliers du Travail of the nineteenth century), was by no means a passive labor organization. On the contrary: its opposition to the so-called international unions, which were in fact American unions, was first and foremost tied to the conservatism of the unions led by Samuel Gompers, who refused to accept non-specialized workers. The core—consisting of national unions—that was the origin of the Confederations of Canadian Catholic Workers and that made the CCCW into a militant organization, as the asbestos strike of 1949, among other things showed—was trying constantly to resist the principles of American unionism for reasons other than mere "nationalism," or "our" nationalism, to use Pierre Elliott Trudeau's expression.

In his text—and we could quote examples *ad nauseam*—Trudeau systematically gives a unidimensional definition to French-Canadian institutions and explains everything by means of the gap between theory and reality. Thus his explanations were limited to caricature, and to an obsession with this "gap." He writes,

> In 1884, Ontario followed English law in setting a minimum age for workers; the following year, Quebec copied the

Ontario law. In 1888 Nova Scotia, in 1894 Ontario and British Columbia, and in 1900 the Federal government adopted the law of voluntary conciliation for industrial disputes; Quebec followed in 1901. In 1900, Ottawa adopted a policy of just salary for federal government workers; a similar law in Quebec was not passed till 1915. In 1900, Ontario encouraged the development of a local paper industry by means of a law forbidding the export of pulp; Quebec followed only in 1910. In 1906, the federal government adopted the Sunday law; the Quebec law on Sunday observance was passed the following year. The federal law on enquiry into industrial inequities (Lemieux Law), adopted in 1907, forbade strikes in a certain number of industries affecting public interest until a public enquiry was held; this law applied to the whole of Canada until it was overturned by a Privy Council decision in 1925; from 1926 to 1932, all provinces except Prince Edward Island extended the federal law to their own jurisdictions; Quebec was the last, in 1932. The Ministry of Labor was created in Ottawa in 1909; British Columbia followed in 1917 and Ontario in 1919; Quebec did not have an independent Ministry of Labor until 1931. Manitoba and British Columbia adopted minimum wage laws for women in 1918; Quebec did so in 1919. In 1919, the Federal government voted in credit payments to encourage the provinces to develop technical and apprenticeship programmes; then in 1928, the provinces adopted apprenticeship programmes; Quebec came in last in 1945. British Columbia began to limit hours of work from 1923; Quebec was second, but ten years later. In 1937 and 1938, four provinces introduced compulsory conciliation of industrial disputes; the equivalent law in Quebec dates from 1944. In 1944, Ontario made paid vacations mandatory; Quebec was the fourth province to adopt a similar law in 1946.[25]

First of all, it should be emphasized that employment laws in English Canada were passed after decades of struggle by English workers and not because England was necessarily "more advanced." Popular pressure in Ontario and Quebec had similar results. And the fact that Quebec "imitated" Ontario "the following year" hardly provides overwhelming proof of social backwardness. That said, Trudeau himself had conceded, earlier in his text, that

> Sometimes it was Quebec that was more innovative than the other provinces. This was the case with our Industrial Accidents Law of 1909, which was based on French law. The following year, Quebec had the first employment offices, based on a 1909 English law pertaining to work subsidies. In 1924, the professional unions of Quebec Law—based on French law of 1884 and 1920—was the first in Canada to give a legal character to trades unions.[26]

All in all, Pierre Elliott Trudeau's analysis of French-Canadian society leaves the reader perplexed, because, among other reasons:

1. he claims that the asbestos strike was a rupture between the people and the "nationalist" élite, whereas in the same breath he says that the people "have never taken any notice" of the élite;

2. after claiming that the people were never taken in by nationalism, he tries to explain Quebec's 'backwardness" by the backwardness of nationalist "thought," which would necessarily have had some currency in that case;

3. finally, he gives a series of empirical examples that do indeed show a relative "backwardness," but nothing that would lead one to think that ideological monolithism could have created a wide—indeed crucial—gap between the "reality" of Quebec and the "reality" of its neighboring societies.

A fourth difficulty should be explained before we consider the question, tackled by Richard Handler in 1988, of whether Quebec was ever monolithic.[27] This fourth difficulty concerns Trudeau's omission of several institutions that did not fit his definition. There is the case of the banks, for example.

In 1985, the historian Ronald Rudin published a study of nine French-Canadian banks between 1895 and 1925: Banque du Peuple, Banque Jacques–Cartier, Banque Ville–Marie, Banque Provinciale, Banque d'Hochelaga, Banque Nationale, Banque de Saint–Hyacinthe, Banque Saint–Jean, and Banque Canadienne Nationale (founded in 1925 following the merge of Banque Nationale and Banque d'Hochelaga). Rudin demonstrated in his enquiry that French-Canadian banks exerted a considerable influence on Quebec society. Two factors in particular marked the evolution of French-Canadian banks: structural changes in the Canadian economy and the linguistic divide that favored small banks in Quebec, at least for a while.[28] From 1835 to 1875, large banks, like the Bank of Montreal, were primarily involved in large-scale trading with England and neglected internal commercial activity. As a result, during this period, several small entrepreneurs, Anglophone or Francophone, opened branches to satisfy the needs of local customers—for instance, the Banque du Peuple in 1833, the Ontario Bank, the Exchange Bank of Dartmouth, and so on. Between 1835 and 1875, the number of banks in British North America rose from eleven to fifty-one and of those, seven were French Canadian.

The situation changed between 1875 and 1921, however. Urbanization and industrialization caused the large banks to take an interest in small capital, which in turn led to a strong tendency to merge: the number of banks in Canada dropped from fifty-one to eighteen between 1875 and 1921. Of these, three French-Canadian banks refused to merge: Banque Nationale, Banque d'Hochelaga, and Banque Provinciale. Between 1901 and 1921, these banks tripled their capital, with ninety-five percent of the new capital coming from French Canadian investors. Initially, the large Anglo-British banks made no particular effort to penetrate the Francophone market, which made French-Canadian banks better able to resist mergers compared to the small and medium-sized Anglophone banks, which were wiped out. This example shows 1) that the French Canadian élite was not necessarily paralysed by "nationalism" to the extent that they remained passive in the face of capitalist moves; and 2) that several factors, among them structural and strategic factors (for example, the decision made by English-speaking administrators not to offer special-ized service to their French-speaking customers), contributed to the reality of a socio-economic network in French Canada. This cannot all be reduced to a mono-causal and unidimen-sional explanation—namely, the gap between nationalist thought and reality. Reality, in fact, was more complex than the version Pierre Elliott Trudeau presented.

To continue. In a work on Quebec business, Yves Bélanger and Pierre Fournier (1987) wrote,

The period 1900–1929 saw the creation of new businesses and some mergers of Francophone Quebec businesses.... A few names stand out, among them the J.J. Joubert Dairy, A. Poupart, Leclerc Dairy, Laval Dairy, Grenache Inc., B. Trudel and Company, etc. Businesses devoted to other areas of agro-food-production also developed, for example J.A. Vachon and son, the Contant Company (Salaison), Kerulu and Oida, Ltd (baked goods), Durivier Inc. (bakery).... In beer production, Frontenac Brewery was a symbol of Quebec industrial success. Founded in 1911 by Joseph Beaubini with a capital of a million dollars, this firm managed to capture the market and even to export its product (from 1912 on). In the tobacco industry, one legendary name stands out: Louis–Ovide Grothé, cigar maker. Founded in 1882, this family business was so successful that it had a budget of several millions of dollars, owned three factories and employed 860 workers.[29]

And so on. Even as Bélanger and Fournier emphasized the relative weakness of the Francophone middle-class, what emerges from their description, perhaps in spite of themselves, is an energy surprising in a middle-class that was repressed by a society marked by its "ideological monolithism." Even the Church was involved:

As we have shown earlier, religious institutions wielded considerable economic power, the fall-out from which benefited a large number of business people. In this context, it was hardly surprising that the biggest manufacturers of organs (Casavant brothers) and of rosaries (Desmarais and Robitaille) would be French. Any discussion of the most famous French Canadian businesses, namely Dupuis Brothers of Montreal and Paquet in Quebec City must take into account the large revenue brought into their coffers by the trade investments generated by all the wearers of the cassock. This was the tip of the iceberg. A considerable number of French Canadian businesses were linked to the Church and its subsidiaries.[30]

The authors further note,

as far as mergers were concerned, they were mainly confined to the manufacturing, construction and transport
sectors. In 1931, these three sectors were controlled by
15,590 owners and managers. In 10 years, this figure had
gone down by 15% and was only 13,283. In addition, these
mergers took place at the expense of Francophones in most
sectors. They not only experienced a decline in their
number in absolute terms, but they also saw their share
shrink dramatically. In 1931, 57% of manufacturing owners
were of French origin; in 1941, this figure was down to 49%.
In the construction industry, there was a similar decline,
the Francophone share falling from 75% to 67%. In the
transport and communications sector, French Canadians
lost a lot of ground going from 78% to 43%.[31]

Bélanger and Fournier are right in concluding that the economic crisis brought with it the disappearance of French-Canadian businesses, although some were absorbed into others owned by Francophones. These few examples show, however, that at the level of the élite, it is hard to prove an ideological monolithism characterized by "distrust of industri-alization, self-reflection, yearning for a return to the land." Even in 1941, according to Bélanger and Fournier's figures, one out of every two manufacturers (forty-nine percent) in Quebec was Francophone. So the "materialism" attributed by Trudeau to the "people" obviously attracted all those thousands of Francophone industrialists who had eagerly gone into business in the first half of the nineteenth century, including, incidentally, Trudeau's own father. How can this obsession with monolithism be explained? The reply has to be given at two levels: on the one hand, there is an important methodological dimension, which will be discussed in the last part of this chapter; on the other hand, there is the political aspect, which will take up the next chapter.

FUNCTIONALISM AND METHODOLOGICAL INDIVIDUALISM

Since the end of the nineteenth century, various theoretical currents have run through sociology, currents which were and remain violently opposed to each other. Beyond labels and categories, these different approaches rest on different principles and fundamentally contradictory bases of interpretation. It is important to give a brief outline of these principles.

Pierre Ansart wrote about the different schools of thought:

> It would be an absurd simplification to reduce the intellectual field of the social sciences to the mere opposition between a theory of socio-economic contradictions and an individualist (or individualizing) theory. Nonetheless, and if we accept for a moment a very general axis of opposition, we can situate this vast intellectual space: on the conflict side authors as disparate as Saint–Simon, Proudhon, Georges Sorel, and authors bordering on Marxism, and on the individualist side, authors as different as M. Weber, V. Pareto, G. Simmer.[32]

Émile Durkheim offered a third epistemological way opposed to these two currents: that of the study of social "phenomena" which are treated like "things" or fundamental elements of the living organism which constitutes society. Thus, in Marxist sociology, what is stressed is the class antagonisms that form the structures of methods of production. In Durkheimian sociology, the object is to create a sociological field distinct from the other social sciences, but epistemologically close to the natural sciences through the study, from a synchronic point of view—that is to say of a precise, determined moment, of "social structure." So Weber, contrary to Durkheim, tried to differentiate the social sciences, and sociology in particular, from the natural sciences by emphasizing the interpretive nature of these disciplines and the necessity of continually bringing the study of social phenomena back to individual strategies.

In 1949, and throughout the 1950s, functionalism exerted an indisputable influence. In the 1950s, in fact, Talcott Parsons' structural functionalism was an essential reference point. But Quebec sociology was modelled to an even greater extent upon notions formulated in the 1930s and 1940s, in particular the notion of function.

At the end of the nineteenth century, Herbert Spencer and Émile Durkheim (Durand and Weil, 1989) used a biological model to describe an organic society forming a whole, all of whose parts have a relationship to the totality. Applied to society, the notion of function was therefore similar to a biological function. Elsewhere, Spencer established the parallel between organic life and social life that he classified under the concept of evolution (Durand and Weil, 1989). According to him, the evolution of a society is characterized by a series of necessary stages, as in the case of living organisms: birth, adulthood, aging.

Contrary to Spencer, Durkheim rejected evolution on stages of development to concentrate on the relationship between the function and the need it fulfills. Durkheim concentrated exclusively on this relationship between need and function from a point of view that was synchronic and based on space at a specific moment, as opposed to diachronic and based on time—therefore history. During the 1930s, Bronislaw Malinowski, using Durkheim's notion of function, also made a study of need and function and defined culture as

the whole corpus of instruments, the privileges of its social groups, the ideas, the beliefs and human customs consti-tute a vast apparatus which places man in a better position to face the specific, concrete problems that confront him during his adaptation to his environment so that he can best satisfy his needs.[33]

During the 1930s, the Chicago School was greatly influ-enced by the idea, dear to "functionalists," of privileging synchronism and not diachronism. The Chicago tradition went back at least to the pragmatists John Dewey and Charles S. Peirce and to the utilitarianism of William James. In this tradi-tion, stress was laid on the experimental method and on the notion that the applicability of concept must be constantly verified and challenged (Durand and Weil, 1989). The socio-logical branch of the Chicago School was disparate, however. It brought together, on the one hand, sociologists like Robert Park, who preferred field-work and the study of dysfunction in urban society, and who rejected theorizing. In this, Park and his disciples looked to Malinowski and the first functionalists for inspiration; they acknowledged, some more than others, the theoretical contribution of Durkheim, but preferred empir-ical enquiry. On the other hand, they differed from Chicago sociologists like Horace Miner, who were influenced by the theories of Radcliffe–Brown and of structural functionalism, which owed an even greater debt to Durkheim. A third group, led by, among others, Robert Redfield, used an evolutionary (and therefore more diachronic) approach to traditional or "folk," peasant, and modern societies. Even with Malinowski and Parks' anti-historic approach, there was an implicit assumption of the sometimes abrupt passage from a pre-industrial to an industrial society. The idea of a historic evolution by stages or of a succession of stages punctuated by crucial turning points, was always there, but never explicit in studies that were concerned exclusively with the organization of society at a precise, and sometimes present moment.

This disparity in points of view could be seen with Miner as well as with Hughes, in the way that Miner, who had done his doctorate under Redfield's direction, nevertheless openly took as his model Radcliffe–Brown's approach; in contrast, Hughes situated his work in the perspective of urban ecology. We have already seen in the introduction that Pierre Elliott Trudeau was making a bid for "functional politics." Elsewhere, in a book we will consider in more detail in the next chapter (Trudeau, 1967), Trudeau declared, after quoting Lord Acton on the unpromising "career" of nationalism, that a new intellectual and political invention could "be functionalism, and will quite clearly appear as inseparable from any viable concept of federalism."[34]

Because Pierre Elliott Trudeau believed that French Canada was suffering from a gap between "thought" and "reality," he subscribed to a functional solution, which required the recognition of a more adequate theory based on the acceptance of modern reality. But we have already seen that neither the people, according to Trudeau himself, nor the élite, according to the evidence we have given, were entirely slaves to nationalist thought—or, that is, to "our" nationalist thought.

At the outset, probably even before he had started doing the research for the first chapter of *The Asbestos Strike*, Trudeau was presumably resolved to describe the collective characteristics of French Canada: the ideologue locked in a struggle against the Duplessis régime became confused with the analyst in search of the essential elements of a collectively described community. But in proposing a transformation of thought in a society that was not yet "adult," Trudeau, far from going against the current, was, on the contrary, both placing himself squarely in the current—dominant in North America—of pragmatic functionalism, and even of evolutionism, since it was clear to the leader of *Cité libre* that French Canada had not yet reached the stage of maturity. How could Trudeau have really gone "against the current"? Or at least, without necessarily going against the current in methodological terms, how could he have posed the problem in the individualist perspective that an author appealing to liberalism should logically have focussed on?

Before examining the individualist perspective, we should note that the sociology of conflict, Marxist in origin, has resulted in the formulation of "dynamic" sociology. Thus, according to Pierre Ansart,

A structuralist approach would tend to make people think that contacts between two societies take place through the collision between two structured systems which can only result in the destruction of the weaker. A more thorough observation shows that a simplistic opposition between "traditional" and "modern" society does not suffice to understand, to take one example, processes of development. On the contrary, in many concrete situations, we should note how the traditional system evolves without being destroyed, how, for example, the founders target "modern" economic objectives using for their own ends the traditional system and villagers' fondness for their customs. The traditional structure does not generate these changes, but the social participants, the leaders, in the face of new economic changes, will use the old structure and uphold it whilst modifying it for their own profit.[35]

Rather than using the somewhat crude perspective of dynamic or conflictual sociology to capture the complex articulation between traditional and modern—which, rather than the sudden, total, and mythic rupture between traditional and modern is the fundamental characteristic of modernity—an author concerned with individualism could have posed the problem of the study of French Canada using the approach known as methodological individualism. Not that this approach is superior in itself, but at least it has the advantage of coherence vis-à-vis the individualist presuppositions of the author. This approach allowed authors—like French sociologists Raymond Boudon and François Bourricaud—to avoid generalizations about "social structures."

At the beginning of the twentieth century, Max Weber pointed out that, "sociology can only proceed from the actions of one, several or many separate individuals. This is why it has to adopt strictly 'individualist' methods."[36] In the same way, philosophers and logicians like Karl Popper blasted the "holistic" theory, which is characterized by "totalizing" explanations and the chimerical search for laws of history and "internal necessity" (Ansart, 1990). This opposition to "holism" was aimed in particular at functionalism, "Marxism, but also any essentialist concept of explanation, making out of an essence the principle of explanations."[37] Trudeau, in establishing at the very beginning the phenomenon of a monolithic, nationalist theory, came pretty near to positing the existence of a French-Canadian "essence." Trudeau also put himself in a position in which it was impossible to see the many dimensions of French Canada, dimensions that resulted from individual strategies on all levels of society. Now, "the objective foregrounded by methodological individualism is situated right there: in an examination of individual behavior within a given social system."[38] Moreover, "methodological individualism, called upon to consider individual behavior and actions, will examine the choices made by the individuals concerned and will formulate hypotheses about these choices."[39] Given that this came from a self-styled champion of individualism like Pierre Elliott Trudeau, and given that attacks against "holism" were virulent even at the time that Trudeau was writing, the reader is dismayed by the total lack of interest shown in *The Asbestos Strike* towards precisely these individual choices. Trudeau seems to have *the* answer before the question has even been asked. Hence we can see that Trudeau's representation of French Canada in *The Asbestos Strike* was essentialist and collectivist, and not individualist. The examples given earlier in this chapter give us a glimpse of a society in which the presupposed "ideological monolithism" had serious cracks. Why? Quite simply because French Canadians, as social agents like those in any other society, did not remain passive, even at the ideological level. In other words, despite the weight of institutions, French Canadians made choices among political values. Thus, in answer to the question whether Quebec was ever monolithic, a much subtler answer could have been formulated, if, among other things, methological individualism had been used. We should point out that such an approach is no guarantee of success. Weber himself, seeking to establish not how capitalism negotiated a path through different religions, but rather how the values of one single religion brought about capitalism, did not apply his own methodological rules, and never answered the question he raised (Disselkamp, 1994). But the application of the principles of methodological individualism could perhaps have allowed Trudeau to grasp a more complex reality. Unfortunately, the same approach, dominated by essentialism as it applied to collectivities and even structures, was used again by Trudeau in *Federalism and French Canadian Society,* which we will examine in the next chapter.

CHAPTER 2
the new betrayal of the intellectuals

"IT ISN'T THE IDEA OF A NATION that's retrograde, it's the idea that a nation must necessarily be sovereign."[1] What a wonderfully acceptable and desirable idea, especially for Quebec! The problem, however, is to articulate it in a non-determinist way in order to make French Canadians in Quebec realize that in history nothing is inevitable or "normal." History, in the sense of a linear process, punctuated by inevitable stages, does not exist. History, on the contrary, defined as an incessant changing of strategies worked out by individuals and groups faced with contexts that are themselves constantly being transformed, is a dynamic, multidimensional reality and is very difficult to interpret. Let us look briefly at how Pierre Elliott Trudeau expressed a vision of the history of nationalism, and, in particular, of French-Canadian nationalism.

FRENCH-CANADIAN AND
ENGLISH-CANADIAN NATIONALISM

Trudeau had this to say about the "modern notion of nation":

> After more than 65 centuries of history, with the break-up of the medieval order, the waning of Latin as the language of the educated man, and the birth of the individualist mystique, the modern notion of nation began to develop in Europe. The replacement of the Catholic Church by national churches, the rise of the bourgeoisie, the protective mercantilism of territorial economies, the outrages committed against certain ethnic groups like the Poles, the Jacobin Revolution, the fervor of Mazzini, the domination of poor nations by industrialized nations like England, these were all factors that contributed to the birth of national aspirations, which in turn were to lead to the successive establishment of national states.[2]

In addition, according to Pierre Elliott Trudeau, at the time of the British conquest,

> the English were already the most nationalistic of men. The entire country, proud of its political and economic superiority, was all in favor of going off to plant its flag, its commerce and its institutions in the most remote lands. This nationalism was necessarily cultural, too, and the English were convinced that the lands conquered by them enjoyed that most undeserved favor: that of being able to commune with the Anglo-Saxon language and culture. Also, the English who put so much skill and political genius into developing the cult of civil liberties at home, never dreamt of protecting minority rights.[3]

Thus, in the nineteenth century, imbued with Anglo-Saxon superiority, "British-Canadian nationalism gave rise, as was inevitable, to French-Canadian nationalism."[4] And quoting himself, Trudeau repeated a key passage published in *The Asbestos Strike*:

> For a conquered, occupied, decapitated people shut out of the commercial domain, driven out of the cities, reduced little by little to a minority, and with diminished influence in a land they had discovered, explored and colonized, there were not many attitudes of mind left which would have allowed them to preserve that which made them themselves. The security system they created around themselves resulted in a stranglehold; in its clutches people sometimes attached too great a price to everything that distinguished them from everybody else, and regarded with hostility any change (even if it were progress) suggested from the outside.[5]

Once again, Pierre Elliott Trudeau seemed more concerned with French-Canadian collectivity than with diversity. Monolithism was *a priori* part of his vision. If guided by a contextualist approach that was more congruent with his liberal vision, Trudeau could no doubt have perceived a more complex dynamic than the monolithism of nationalist thought. But this was not the case. Global judgements continued to mark his texts:

> that this [British] nation might one day be able to afford the luxury of choosing "freely" a destiny more or less the same as the one it's been fighting against. But it would be an unmitigated tragedy not to see that the French-Canadian nation is too culturally anemic, too economically impover-

ished, too intellectually retarded, too spiritually paralysed to be able to survive one or two decades of stagnation during which it will have poured *all* its strength into the cesspool of national vanity and "dignity."[6]

Now according to French writer Julien Benda, who was the inspiration for the title and various elements of the text, a scholar or an intellectual commits an act of betrayal, when, for fear of the consequences, he deliberately omits to tell the truth. So Benda himself had no hesitation in supporting Dreyfus, socialism, the Spanish Republicans. In the view of this harsh critic of Bergson, the great champion of rationalism and order (to the point of venerating the army), the whole of society was becoming secular, including the Catholic intellectuals who were cravenly yielding to national necessity. So for Benda, the ultimate traitor from the intellectual point of view was someone like Maurice Barrès, who is reported to have said, "even if our country is wrong, we must think it is right."[7]

Very well. But what happens when through the spectacles of the intellectual who doesn't want to be a traitor and who still wants to tell the truth, one encounters the stare of the Other, who is dominant, and who has a tendency to reduce everything? Trudeau took to task Quebec "monolithism" but at the same time his own view of the society was itself "monolithic."

For Pierre Elliott Trudeau, the Quiet Revolution marked Quebec's entry into modernity, a modernity characterized by the absolute triumph of liberty. Thus, "the generation that was reaching its twenties in 1960 was the first in our history that had more or less total and unadulterated freedom."[8] Really? But if liberty is universal, why would it be less so in a specific period? Why would French Canadians have been incapable of exercising their liberty in all its complexity before 1960? Pierre

Elliott Trudeau had maintained that historically, English-Canadian nationalism had consisted in not wanting liberty for others, and for French Canadians in not wanting it for themselves. But such a proposition implies that Trudeau, while running down English-Canadian nationalism, was himself taking over the dominating view of some English Canadians as he looked at French Canadians: namely that liberalism, prerogative of the British, was incompatible with French Canada. Now Anglo-American culture had been dominated for two centuries by the idea of Anglo-American superiority, thanks to a precocious modernization that was brought about by the natural "laws" of evolution (Spencer held this very view). From this perspective, the Quiet Revolution was seen by some as a historic move into modernity, which was very belated compared with advanced societies. Since Pierre Elliott Trudeau made an enormous contribution to working out this interpretation, we should take a moment to situate it in the historiography of the last decades and in the interpretations of France and England since the eighteenth century.

THE REPRESENTATION OF QUEBEC SINCE THE NEW BETRAYAL OF THE INTELLECTUALS

Pierre Elliott Trudeau's representation of Quebec in *The New Betrayal of the Intellectuals,* and in his chief writings, has become canonical.[9] On 4 May 1996, for example, Lysiane Gagnon wrote in the *Globe and Mail* (1996),

The difference, apart from the ocean of differences that separates Europe from North America, is that in France, civil society cut its ties with the Church more than 200 years ago, after the French Revolution in 1789. Since then, an elaborate secular ethic has developed, with a set of moral values and traditions that provides social stability. Québec, on the other hand, is still shaking from the tremor of its Quiet Revolution.

The image of a so-called traditional society, dominated by the Church, as the quote from Lysiane Gagnon shows, is still widespread in the Canadian media and seems to be accepted by the public, both English-speaking and French-speaking. Elsewhere, in texts published in 1988 and 1994, historian Jocelyn Létourneau has clearly represented the collective and historic imaginary construct of young Quebeckers who associate the Lesage régime and the Quiet Revolution

> with ideas of progress, modernization, gaining ground and a Golden Age. On the other hand, they identify Duplessis, his régime and his working-class politics with the Quebec "Middle Ages," with the "Dark Ages," with fanatical anti-labor and anticommunism, with authoritarianism and autocracy.

Further on, we find, according to Létourneau,

> in several ways, the reasoning seems modelled on a teleological view of the history and structures of Quebec according to a political mythology the principal terms of which are: conspiracy, savior and Golden Age.[10]

By virtue of this teleological view,

> Duplessis is a conservative, a friend of the capitalists, an anti-unionist, a dictator; he "reigns" over a traditional, slumbering, immobile, self-absorbed, paralysed society, a society of the "Dark Ages" literally offered up to foreign capital.[11]

This historic and evolutive imaginary construct is in stark contrast to the development of the social sciences in Quebec and in Canada, and in particular to the historiography of recent years. According to Ronald Rudin, in a text published for the first time in 1992 in the *Canadian Historical Review* and republished in French in the *Bulletin d'histoire politique*, the new historiography "dominant" at the moment states that Quebec society was "normal" and that "the past could be understood by means of the processes common to the West such as urbanization and industrialization" (Rudin, 1994). According to Rudin, however, this new historiography coincided with the articulation of a project of modern society that was characteristic of the dominant discourse of the 1970s and 1980s in Quebec. Rudin draws a parallel between Irish historiography of the 1960s, which was also seeking normality, and Quebec historiography—or writing about Quebec—in the 1970s and 1980s. Rudin finds it regrettable that the new historiography, with the exception of Fernande Roy, has not followed the example of the Irish historian Cormac O'Grada in constructing a balanced interpretation—in the sense of a balance between the old orthodoxy and the new interpretations. He writes, "Revisionists in Quebec have appeared reluctant to admit to the unique aspects of the province's past that might conflict with its newfound image as a modern, vibrant and pluralistic society."[12]

Yet in the text of the Declaration of Sovereignty presented in October 1995 and signed, among others, by the late sociologist Fernand Dumont, politician Henri Brun, poet Gilles Vigneault, and playwright Marie Laberge, it is impossible to detect the slightest trace of this historiography, since Quebec history is presented from an exclusively teleological point of view: punctuated by necessary stages and a moment of salvation, in this case the Quiet Revolution. According to this linear view of history, the next "normal" stage can thus only be sovereignty.

But what is a "normal" society? What is a "normal" historical process? From the philosophical point of view, American philosopher Richard Rorty, in a book entitled *Philosophy and the Mirror of Nature* (1979), calls into question the idea that it is possible to form a judgement about our beliefs based on an objective point of view. Following on from this problematic, we might ask whether it is possible for the social sciences to construct a transcendent universal model from specific contexts and strategies.

So exactly which society can be identified as a universal model in order to compare and contrast Quebec's backwardness? Inasmuch as French Canada developed from a colonizing society which became colonized, how is the relationship between the view of the British colonizer and the view of their own society of the French/Quebec-Canadians to be articulated? How is the apparently large gap between the collective and historical imaginary construct that Quebeckers adhere to today and the work of this new historiography to be explained?

If the new historiography of the last twenty years seems not to have made a substantial change in general public perception, some of the theories developed by social scientists and historians between 1930 and 1970 have certainly played a key role in the formulation of this imaginary construct built around the concept of a traditional society that is said to have existed before the Quiet Revolution.

THE SOCIAL SCIENCES AND CONTEMPORARY QUEBEC: SOCIOLOGY

In one way, as we have seen, the image of contemporary Quebec was first created in the work of the American sociologists of the 1930s associated with the "Chicago School," who influenced the Quebec sociologists of the mid-twentieth century (Couture and Denis, 1994). These sociologists, particularly Hubert Guindon, Jean-Charles Falardeau, and Marcel Rioux, crystallized in their interpretations the image of a fundamentally traditionalist society shoved by modernity into the twentieth century during the Quiet Revolution.

To sum up, the objective of these authors was to capture the elements of French-Canadian society from a synchronic angle at the moment of its dissolution due to the effects of industrialization and urbanization. The plan of the evolution of this society is the following, which is also to be found, implicitly or explicitly, in Trudeau's texts (Couture, 1991 and 1994):

- during the period of New France, French Canada reproduced to a large degree the structures of pre-Revolutionary France, mainly centered on community, parish, pre-capitalist mentality;

- following the Conquest, French Canadians, deprived of privileged contact with the English metropolis, turned to "self-subsistence agriculture," which stressed a tendency to give priority to pre-Revolutionary, pre-capitalist values;

- following the Act of Constitution in 1791, the formation of a French-Canadian nationalism which had responsible government as its main theme, came to an end with the failure of the patriotic movement of 1837–38;

- this failure precipitated the marginalisation of French Canadians in the area of trade and reinforced the power of the dominant Catholic bureaucracy at the end of the 1860s, namely a few years after Confederation;

- the Catholic bureaucracy was therefore responsible for the preservation of a conservation ideology centered on faith, tradition, agriculturism, and anti-materialism just at the moment of the development of modern capitalism, which was characterized by urbanization and, obviously, industrialization;

- upset by these phenomena, the dominant values of French-Canadian society were eroded little by little until they collapsed during the Quiet Revolution in the 1960s.

This last proposition was obviously developed by Quebec sociologists who lived through the Quiet Revolution. The American sociologists were fascinated by acculturation, that is to say, by the encounter between a modern Anglo-American culture and a "traditional" French-Canadian culture.

POLITICAL SCIENCE

Although they used different concepts, political scientists developed a similar interpretation of French-Canadian society. One approach, which although it was not necessarily dominant (Forbes, 1987) was widely taken up in political science literature, was known as the fragment theory or Hartzian model. This theory, which was worked out by Louis Hartz in the 1950s for a study of the United States (1955), was taken up in Canada by authors like Kenneth McRae (1964), Gad Horowitz (1971), André J. Bélanger (1974), and, at least implicitly, by Pierre Elliott Trudeau (1967). The key concept of Hartzian theory is the "ideological fragment." At the time of European colonization of the world in the sixteenth century, Europe constituted an ideological whole formed of two principal fragments: the community/feudal fragment and the individualist fragment. These two fragments subsequently formed reference points in an ideological spectrum composed, from left to right, of socialism, radical liberalism, "Whig" liberalism, "Tory" conservatism, and feudalism. Depending on their moment of origin and the particular ideological situation of their metropolis at the time of colonization, the new societies created in the United States, Canada, Latin America, and Australia developed a culture based on one of the principal ideological fragments. In the United States, for example, the individualist ideological fragment associated with the thought of the philosopher John Locke (hence the use of the expression "Lockean fragment") was so dominant after the American Revolution that it became the essential dimension of American society. On the other hand, in French Canada and Latin America, the absence of real liberal revolutions led to the perpetuation of the "feudal/community" fragment. In other words, colonial societies of Anglo-Saxon origin, including English Canada, were "Lockean"; the others, including French Canada, remained "feudal." There was no unanimity about the interpretation of English Canada (Forbes, 1987), or if there was, the interpretation was colored by the theory of the civic humanism of the Italian Renaissance (Ajzenstat and Smith, 1995); yet the political scientists who used the theory recognized, for the most part (except Forbes), the "feudal" nature of French Canada.

HISTORIOGRAPHY AND THE PRE-REVOLUTIONARY MENTALITY

In history, Donald Creighton and Fernand Ouellet took up the idea of a pre-Revolutionary mentality attributed to French Canadians. The latter seem to have preserved the values of pre-Revolutionary France right up to the twentieth century. Centered on tradition and community, this mentality seemed particularly incompatible with the spirit of capitalism that was so well developed among Anglo-American Protestants.

For Creighton, who had studied the history of the 1789 Revolution with Mathias (Berger, 1977) in France itself, French Canadians were a systematic obstacle to the realization of the main project of the Montreal Anglophone bourgeoisie after the Conquest, of making Montreal the basic economic axis of North America. Dominated as they were by the Church and held back by their attachment to the past, they were incapable of facing the challenges of modern capitalism.

In his work, historian Fernand Ouellet (1965) took up essentially the same thesis, which he integrated with the prestigious methodological apparatus of quantitative social history that had come out of the Annales school. Ouellet refined the hypothesis of the pre-Revolutionary mentality by trying to show a correlation between the enforcement of nationalism and economic crises: because they were incapable of facing the conjectural challenges of capitalism, French Canadians reacted by clinging to traditional structures. The mental structures of the pre-Revolutionary period were both a fundamental cause of the French Canadians' incapacity to adapt to capitalism and an amplified consequence of conjectural problems.

As far as the new historiography is concerned, and contrary to what Rudin has written, most of these authors have not been frantically trying to find traces of "normality" in French-Canadian society, but have, for the most part, simply reproduced to the letter the dominant propositions about French Canada from history and social science: ideological monolithism—in the sense of the single presence of a so-called traditionalist ideology; the almost total lack of a middle class; the regression to an agriculture of self-subsistence; the perpetuation of the values of pre-Revolutionary France. Examination of these propositions, once again taken absolutely literally, has led to refinements in the presentation of the scenario of the transformation of French-Canadian society since the Conquest:

- After 1763, the French who stayed in America did not regress to an agriculture of self-subsistence. Studies (Courville, Séguin) on the French-Canadian rural world reveal a highly developed economy as early as the turn of the eighteenth to nineteenth centuries with a surprisingly dynamic complex of local and provincial markets, which is in complete contrast to the immobile rural world described by researchers into pre-Revolutionary France.

- At least since the beginning of the nineteenth century, and in spite of the obstacles created by a change of metropolis in the context of a mercantile economy, some French Canadians managed to integrate themselves into Anglo-Saxon commercial networks, whereas others concentrated on developing French-Canadian economic networks, especially in the banking sector.

- After 1840, the Church, it is true, became more and more powerful, whereas the radical liberal current founded by the Patriots was marginalised. But a so-called classic liberal current developed alongside the ideological influence of the Church, without either of these two social and political forces making a systematic effort to oppose progress.

- The result was that during the period 1850 to 1950, French Canada, although a conservative society, was not a traditional monolithic society. French Canada certainly had its specific characteristics, but these are not sufficient to posit the existence of a "folk" society.

Now let us remember that Robert Redfield (1947) had defined "folk society" as a demographically stable society with a technologically under-developed, rural economy, deeply religious to the point where religious interests always dominate secular ones and in which the transformation of work always takes place within the family. In the case of French Canada, these characteristics were inherited from pre-Revolutionary France that is, France before 1789, which is defined as non-industrial.

An understanding of the economic situation in eighteenth century France is important in that the perception of this reality was a key element in the interpretation of the consequences of the Conquest for French Canada. According to Philippe Garigue (1971), however, French Canada was never a rural society because feudalism in New France was very different from the feudal system in the metropolis. In North America, peasants were more independent and did not have to support the entire weight of the injustices imposed by privilege in France. On the contrary, as we know, for Rioux and Guindon (1964) and pretty much so for Hartz (1955), New France was a subculture of France; with the Conquest, French Canadians had no choice but to reinforce the characteristics of rural society by shutting themselves away in subsistence agriculture where the market had little importance. But what was the situation in France in the eighteenth century? What exactly was this society of which New France was thought to be a replica in miniature?

To start with, to understand the ways in which France differed from England, we should keep sight of a few basic facts. France was a country of between twenty-five and twenty-six million inhabitants on the eve of the Revolution, compared with eight million in England (Verley, 1985). Essentially a continental power, France had, nonetheless, overtaken England in industry and commerce in the eighteenth century (Crouzet, 1985). According to François Crouzet (1967), between 1720 and 1780, French merchants ousted British merchants from the continent and made significant inroads in the West Indies, especially in the sugar industry. In total, during those sixty years, French global trade quintupled. In other areas, according to the same sources, coal production in France increased by 700% during those same years, compared to 279% in England. Iron and steel production over the same period increased by 468% in France, as opposed to 100% in England.

As a result, New France was not "less feudal" merely because of the North American surroundings and the wide open spaces, but also because many of the French who came to the Saint Laurence Valley were the products of a metropolis that was engaged in lively capitalism despite the juridical domination of the aristocracy.

It is inconceivable that mid-eighteenth century England could be seen as an already industrialized nation, way ahead of France. The Industrial Revolution, which began in the cotton spinning industry between 1760 and 1820, reached other sectors (weaving, woolens, railways) only between 1820 and 1850. But even there, French backwardness was relative, since between 1815 and 1840 (Verley, 1885) the annual rate of global industrial growth was 3.4% in France as opposed to 3.8% in England. In fact, the actual supremacy of England lasted from 1850 to 1889, the years when the United States rose to first in the world in industrial production. It is important, therefore, to relativise England's economic advance (Crouzet, 1985). On the other hand, differences in the social area are more significant. In France, the role of the bourgeoisie is very controversial (Bétourné, Hartig, 1989). Was the Revolution really the victory of the bourgeoisie it was claimed to be, especially if we consider the fact that there had been, to a certain extent, economic preparation for such an event? Once again, we should do a comparative study of different features. Certainly, on 10 August 1789, the old order was legally abolished. And on 26 August 1789, the Declaration of the Rights of Man and the Citizen consecrated the victory of the philosophy of natural rights, the basis for the respect of fundamental rights.

In 1791, the first constitution issued from the revolution of 1789, with its suffrage of property owners, marked the triumph of the English model of democracy, namely élitist and aristocratic. This came about because at the beginning of the Revolution, many of the aristocrats and bourgeois in favor of change had in mind the English model of the constitution that had come out of the Glorious Revolution of 1688. However, during the second phase of the Revolution, the movement became radicalized in France to the point where some of the instigators of 1789 became victims of the Reign of Terror. In addition, the bourgeoisie of the old régime was massacred during the Terror. And after 1795, a new middle class appeared. The French army, which went from 225,000 men in 1792 to 1,000,000 in 1796, offered a substantial market for producers of arms, cast iron, and clothing, as well as for agricultural producers (Verley, 1985).

Thus in France, after the economic disaster of 1789–1795, growth began again in 1795, and there was a significant rallying between 1802 and 1814. At the end of the Napoleonic Wars, French industrial production exceeded by fifty percent that of 1789 (Woronoff, 1988). And it was mainly the new middle class who gained from this rallying. In Lyon, for example, in 1807, seventy-four percent of tradesmen were new to the world of trade, having entered it after 1795–96 (Bonin, 1985).

This new middle class survived the Napoleonic period and the Restoration to reach, with the July Monarchy (1830), an important socio-political compromise with part of the revived aristocracy and independent members of the peasantry. Consensus was reached in terms of social order and economic progress. The new middle class began to imitate the lifestyle of the aristocracy and argued in favor of tradition, all the while investing in trade and industry. As for the independent peasantry, according to Robert Bates (1998), they formed a source of stability and a consumer base necessary for economic growth in the French context. In short, the rise of capitalism took place without the French peasants being crushed, whereas an inverse situation prevailed in England. There, the new class of agricultural journeymen created by the "enclosures" was severely repressed (Couture, 1993).

To sum up, there were several different routes of access to capitalism which resulted in specific social strategies and complex policies in each country. The idea that French Canada was built on the global values of pre-capitalist France is too mechanical an intellectual construction to account for this complexity.

ENGLAND

In England, the Industrial Revolution as such was largely the work of small tradesmen and yeomen who rushed into the production of cotton thread at the end of the eighteenth century. The English middle class of the Industrial Revolution, the class of cotton manufacturers and later of promoters of the railway (Crouzet, 1985), was essentially a new middle class. Yet throughout the first third of the nineteenth century, these newly rich and the great families of English tradespeople had access to political life through the Reform Bill of 1832, which raised the number of voters in England from 432,000 to 712,000 (Tousignant, 1973).

In other words, according to Guttsman (1965) and Rubinstein (1976), England remained throughout the nine-

teenth century a country socially dominated by the old aristocratic élite who were able to impose and preserve their élitist
political institutions. In fact, at the time of the Industrial
Revolution, the new middle class had no other social and
political aims than to be co-opted by the old élite. The stability
of the old English aristocracy—and herein lies the difference
with France—stemmed from its victory during the revolutions
of the seventeenth century. Whereas in France the aristocracy
was defeated during the Fronde and absolutism was
entrenched, in England the aristocrats took over power in
1688. Now the ideology, or world view, of this élite, which was
not middle class, was classic liberalism, masterfully expressed
by the two Treatises on Civic Government by John Locke.
Perhaps classic liberalism has been too often associated with
the middle class (André Vachet, 1970), whereas, in fact, it was
developed before the Industrial Revolution and above all
offered a justification of the world view and values of a land-
owning élite. Most of these land-owners did, indeed, take up
intensive agriculture during the seventeenth and eighteenth
centuries. But at the time of the Industrial Revolution *per se*,
very few of these aristocrats participated directly in the
change. On the contrary, certain absolutely classic liberals like
Edmund Burke (Macpherson, 1980) condemned industrial
capitalism and the threat it represented for the community
(Nisbet, 1984). Even at this level, "monolithism" is nowhere in
sight.

On the other hand, with the intensive development of this
kind of capitalism in the nineteenth century, some aristocrats
and most of the industrial middle class justified the economic
change in social stability by a view of the world characterized
by the predominance of private property and liberal political
institutions completely controlled by "land-owners" alone.
(Macpherson, 1980). Throughout the nineteenth century, and

even up to the first World War, middle-class and aristocratic English males could function within political institutions conceived in the seventeenth century by aristocrats for aristocrats. According to Arno Mayer (1983) and Yves Lequin (1978), this persistence of the old régime was the major characteristic of the nineteenth century. Even Durkheim, uneasy about the dissolution of the community in the modern world, was forced to acknowledge that in England—albeit a country in which the organic solidarity, which is a trademark of modern societies, should have been easy to achieve—there were still large "segments" of tradition even at the turn of the twentieth century (Aron, 1967).

In short, although France and England presented different social configurations (Stone, 1985; Levi, 1988; Bates, 1988) and an equally different dynamic of development, these two countries had in common their experience of the Industrial Revolution without tradition and modernity being necessarily in conflict. Quite the reverse, in fact. In addition, England has too often been held up in literature and the social sciences as a universal case, to such an extent that authors today denounce the "perfidy" of English "universalism" characterized by the triumph of the upper-middle class and the disappearance of the rural-working class as necessary for modernization (Bates, 1988). Other authors go so far as to call into question the validity of the model for England itself (Stone, 1985; Crafts, 1983; Williamson, 1984; Bedarida, 1974). As for the United States, it should be remembered that the Federalists of the end of the eighteenth century, great champions of an administratively and financially centralized America, were also defenders of the European tradition of order and authority (Appleby, 1984).

Now that these details about France and England have been established, we should bring out another important aspect of Anglo-American culture: historicism and the "Whig" conception of history.

THE ANGLO-AMERICAN MODEL AND "WHIGISM"

In one way, all three of the disciplines (history, sociology, political science) we have been concerned with were influenced, directly or indirectly, by what Sir Herbert Butterfield described in 1932 as a Whig interpretation of history. This vision of history, developed in the eighteenth century by Edmund Burke in his writings about the French Revolution, and again in the nineteenth century by the historians Carlyle and Macaulay, is historicist in the sense that it constitutes a linear representation of a history determined by tradition and natural evolution. The natural evolution of English society made it into a society where liberty won out against "community" and feudalism. Since history is an unceasing battle between Progress and Obscurantism, it was incumbent upon the enlightened English aristocracy to see that liberty triumphed first of all in England and then throughout the world. The Whig conception of history, therefore, rests on the universality of the English model of development. It was also defined in reaction to the French Revolution by Burke, of course, but also by Carlyle, whose first important publication was a history of the French Revolution published in the very year 1837. As for Macaulay, his history of England, published between 1849 and 1855, aimed to show the superiority of the English institutions that had sprung from the 1688 Revolution in relation to the French Revolution. Only a natural evolution was a guarantee of progress, maintained Macaulay; the French Revolution, on the other hand, with its desire to impose reason in the face of nature, perpetuated obscurantism. Macaulay's history of England was the biggest bestseller of the Victorian age and has been republished every year to the present (Drabble, 1995).

This interpretation constitutes the cornerstone of Creighton's theory about the mentality of pre-Revolutionary France and is also central to the Hartzian theory of the ideological fragment. Its influence on sociology was more indirect. We have already seen that the approach used by the sociologists of the Chicago School was intended to be synchronic, as opposed to the diachronic perspective of the large-scale evolutive syntheses—Spencer's, for example. Yet the synchronism of the structural functionalism characteristic of the approach of the sociologists of the Chicago School in the 1930s rests, as we have already seen, on the assumption of an abrupt passage from the pre-industrial world to the industrial, urban world, Anglo-American societies being by definition marked to a much greater degree by the modern world. Thus, the evolutive schema, for want of being explicitly recognized, became implicitly incorporated into the synchronic approach of the Chicago School. At first sight, this schema as it is reiterated in the twentieth century in such classic works as those of Barrington Moore and Theda Skocpol, rests on the idea of the triumph of the English middle class from the seventeenth century on, thus paving the way for the Industrial Revolution of the eighteenth century.

Now, we have already indicated that there was no consensus about the universality of the English case among economic historians, even if it is still the fundamental principle of the analyses done in economics and finance (Disselkamp, 1994; Verley, 1985; Lequin, 1978). An entire literature has grown up questioning the idea of the "precocious" development of the English middle class which paved the way for modern capitalism (Disselkamp, 1994). If the universality of the English case is seriously undermined (Polanyi, 1983;

Mayer, 1983; Lequin, 1978), it still stands as a constant reference, especially as this century ends, at the time of the globalization of the market-place. We are witnessing, in fact, not the end of ideologies (Fukuyama, 1991), but rather the triumph of a reductionist ideology based on the Anglo-American model. One of the most fascinating socio-political and cultural phenomena of the last two centuries was the domination of Anglo-American culture expressed through a historicist vision formed on the basis of the idea that England and the United States were the first, and perhaps the only countries, to develop an individualist society, as opposed to all other societies, which were "community based." The work of Louis Hartz expressed this idea perfectly clearly. A certain Anglo-Saxon culturalist nationalism developed mainly through this vision of history which is often accepted by the intellectuals of other countries. Trudeau was certainly no exception to this phenomenon.

FRENCH CANADA AND ORIENTALISM

This last observation poses the problem of language and discourse, and in particular, the principle that all discourse is a form of power, as outlined first by Frantz Fanon, then by Michel Foucault. In *Orientalism* (1978), Edward Said took up this principle and maintained that the Orient had been a creation of the Western colonizer. On the pretext that the Orient was unable to represent itself, the West gave itself a monopoly on representation. Thus the Orient allowed the West to define itself by means of contrast: defining the Other was an exercise in self-definition. But the problem of the representation of the colonized conceals the problem of the presentation of the colonizers themselves. If, as Jean–François Lyotard has written, "to speak is to fight" (1979), then the representation of the colonized by the colonizer necessarily implies a definition of a relationship of force which precludes the colonizers' integrating their own contradictions. Besides, colonizers from a specific country are themselves competing with other colonialist countries, and must position themselves not only in relation to the colonized but also in relation to colonizing rivals. This is where the case of French Canada presents a fascinating, and perhaps unique, example. Forming a society that was at first colonizing then colonized, the French of North America, who became French Canadians, and after the Quiet Revolution—for those living in Quebec—Quebeckers, were at the frontier of two great western cultures, but also formed, right in the heart of the West, a society whose status as dominated since the Conquest of 1760 was also defined as a function of the positioning of one colonizer vis-à-vis another.

DECONSTRUCTION AND COLONIALISM

In order to elaborate on this last comment, let us examine the way Frantz Fanon (1961) described the dominated/colonized intellectual:

1) during the early phase, colonized intellectuals assimilate the literary production and the intellectual tradition of the colonizing country;

2) during the second phase, refusal to assimilate leads to an idealized and romantic representation of the past, all of this still articulated within the philosophic and intellectual traditions of the colonizer;

3) finally, during the third phase, the colonized intellectuals return to their own tradition through involvement in political activism.

From this perspective, it is interesting to observe the extent to which many French-Canadian or Francophone Quebec intellectuals—since the 1960s—both participated in the events of the Quiet Revolution and contributed to the definition of the society of the "dark ages." In doing this, they situated the "liberation" of Quebec—and not of French Canada—in the very area of the representation of a society dominated by the dominator/colonizer. Hence the following paradoxes and the "perverse effects" to use the terminology of methodological individualism:

1) For more than thirty years, federalists and sovereigntist nationalists have used the same diagnosis of the traditional and backward nature of French-Canadian society before 1960; in both cases, they define the Quiet Revolution as the moment of salvation in an evolutive historic process which finally allowed Quebec to catch up with the Anglo-Saxon world on the linear historic ladder. The only thing that distinguishes the two currents is the conclusion of history: in one case ,the final liberation has already taken place with the institutions of the Trudeau era; for others, only sovereignty can constitute normal "liberation." Thus, the more sovereignty is defined as a function of an Anglo-American historicist perspective, the more it contributes to the internalization of a certain Anglo-American view in Quebec by Quebeckers themselves.

2) If discourse about the "dark ages" allowed Quebeckers to achieve their liberty—to become emancipated—in the sense that a rejection of the past has encouraged the blossoming of greater self-confidence, this came about, as has already been emphasized, within the logic of a representation heavily influenced by the Anglo-American view. By now this repre-

sentation is so thoroughly entrenched on the level of cultural practice that it constitutes an insurmountable obstacle to any more subtle assessment of the complexity of the past and of French-Canadian or Quebec society. In addition, reducing the complexity of French-Canadian culture casts a shadow on the complexity of the relationship between tradition and modernity that lies at the heart of Anglo-American society (including English Canada). We have already shown that if there has been a common norm or principle in western societies over the last two centuries, it has nothing to do with the universal nature of English evolutionism; rather, it is in the principle of a complex articulation of traditional and modern, without an abrupt break. In the last text he wrote before his death, Michel Foucault (1984) remarked, pertinently,

> Referring to Kant's text, I wonder whether we could not see modernity rather as an attitude than as a period in history....And consequently, rather than trying to distinguish the "modern period" from "pre" or "postmodern," I believe we would be better off investigating how it is that the attitude of modernity, since its formation, has been in a confrontational situation with the attitudes of anti-modernity.[13]

Understanding modernity means bringing out the multiple dimensions of the articulation of tradition-modernity.

3) The new historiography has not gained acceptance, at least with the general public, for the simple reason that the political stakes are too high. On the one hand, recognizing the multidimensional aspect of French Canada before the Quiet Revolution would, in the long run, open up the possibility of calling into question the universality of the

Anglo-American model. A key element of Anglo-American culture could therefore collapse, which many specialists in English Canada are not prepared to countenance.

But on the other hand, deconstruction of the myth of the "dark ages" is unacceptable to the sovereigntists as well: we know that a key element in Anglo-American—especially British—representation is in fact a reductionist representation of pre-Revolutionary France. What we are dealing with here is the relationship between one colonizer and another. To recognize this aspect is to recognize the fact that French Canada was a relatively colonized society with a status absolutely unlike that of Third World peoples, and that the process of national liberation does not automatically and necessarily involve the formation of a nation-state. Nothing is inevitable, and from the intellectual point of view, an "adult" people could very well decide to belong to a federation. On this point, Trudeau was absolutely right. But the utterly determinist and historicist way he articulated his vision of French Canada totally contradicted the idea of diversity in a collectivity. On the contrary, a century before Trudeau, a French-Canadian intellectual was in a position to express that diversity and to articulate the relationship between liberalism and nationalism within French-Canadian society itself. This intellectual was Étienne Parent.

CHAPTER 3
Étienne Parent

a liberal thinker one century before
Pierre Elliot Trudeau

WRITING ABOUT ÉTIENNE PARENT,[1] Gérard Bergeron asked, "why ... is Parent unknown to the present generation?"[2] The reply—even a cursory reply—to that question has to take into account the phenomenon of the Quiet Revolution. As we have seen in chapters one and two, since the 1960s, history and social science have played a major, if not essential, role in the representation of the so-called traditional society that existed before the Quiet Revolution. The public in general and many specialists even today persist in seeing pre-1960 French Canada as a society dominated by a traditionalist Church, which set against the capitalist, urban, and industrial society of the nineteenth and twentieth centuries the values of pre-industrial, pre-Revolutionary France.[3] This has resulted in limiting interest in non-traditionalist currents of thought since 1960 and into the 1980s. This probably accounts for the fact that Étienne Parent, who was considered a liberal thinker, was not given the place and importance due to him. In the interests of bringing out the ambiguities in Trudeauist thought, it is important to describe the way an author like Étienne Parent articulates liberalism and nationalism. But first, we should remind our readers who Étienne Parent was.

ÉTIENNE PARENT

Étienne Parent was born on 2 May 1802 in Beauport.[4] He was the eldest son of Étienne–François Parent and Josèphe Clouet, who had fifteen children, nine of them boys. The first "Parent," native of Montagne in the Perche province of France, arrived in America in 1634.[5] At the beginning of the nineteenth century, the Parent family belonged to a more or less impoverished rural élite and was probably illiterate.[6]

After completing his primary school studies in Beauport, and perhaps in Quebec, young Étienne was sent to the Collège de Nicolet in 1814 to complete his education.[7] Among his classmates at Nicolet were Charles–François Baillargeon (future Bishop of Quebec) and Pierre–Horace Panet.[8] In 1819, he continued his studies at the Quebec Seminary, where he met Augustin–Norbert Morin (1803–1865). The seminary seems to have been run by very pro-British teachers,[9] just like the Collège de Nicolet.[10] No doubt there was some logic in the fact that the members of the clergy who loathed revolutionary and Napoleonic France would be great admirers of the aristocratic and monarchic liberalism of Great Britain. This phenomenon was a tremendously important factor in the education of the young Parent, but also for many French-Canadian liberals of the nineteenth century.

In 1821, for apparently unexplained reasons, Étienne Parent left the seminary before taking his final exams.[11] He worked for a while in the hardware shop of his uncle, Michel Clouet, before returning to the family farm. In the meantime, political life in Lower Canada was constantly shaken by disagreements between the Assembly, on the one hand, and the Governor and his advisors on the other.[12] In 1817, Louis Papineau and John

Picture from Le Répertoire National *by James Huston* (*National Archives of Canada and Collection Bibeau*)

Neilson had re-launched *Le Canadien* so that they could reply to the diatribes of the Government party. This journal had been founded in 1806 by Pierre Bédard and François Blanchet, then closed in 1810 on the orders of Governor Craig.[13] The second series of *Le Canadien* was published from 14 June 1817 to 15 December 1819. After a brief interruption, a third series came out on 19 January 1820 and at the beginning of 1821; Augustin–Norbert Morin was the editor. Then Morin left Quebec to go to Montreal to study law. At that point, *Le Canadien* was without an editor-in-chief, and in 1822 the owner, François Blanchet, and the acting editor, François Mallerand, went "in person," according to the legend, to meet Étienne Parent in Beauport.[14] One fact remains: an editorial note in May 1822 announced that the board had found an editor "capable" of guiding the journal.

Before expressing profound Americanism and enthusiasm for economic liberalism in 1846 and 1847, Étienne Parent was right at the heart of the debates and political discussions of the 1820s and 1830s. As soon as he became editor of *Le Canadien,* he had his first fight over the project of the union of the two Canadas.[15]

When the imperial metropolis had created two distinct colonies, Upper and Lower Canada, in 1791, it had done so with the intention of letting the Loyalists of the Lake Ontario region develop a colony without fear of the presence of a French majority. In this way, both colonies had a legislative assembly without any real sovereignty. This system created bitter animosity in the two colonies between, on the one hand, the group of civil servants, aristocrats, and middle-class people who surrounded the governors and their councils, and on the other, the elected representatives of the Assembly who were demanding the application of the principle of responsible government for their colony. The conflict had a further dimension in Lower Canada, given the opposition between the colonial Administration with an English-speaking majority and the Assembly with a French-speaking majority. One of the solutions to the conflict was to join the two colonies, in order to reduce the Francophone majority of Lower Canada—even to reduce it to a minority, ultimately. At the beginning of 1823, Parent launched a violent attack against this project in *Le Canadien* and supported the petition taken to London by Louis–Joseph Papineau and John Neilson.[16] The project was finally abandoned without any solution to the question of responsible government.

It must not be forgotten, however, that Parent and the other political leaders of French Canada continued to "cherish" the

Constitution of 1791: "happy in our misfortune if only we are allowed to keep, from this constitution which we so rightly cherish, the meaningless name...."[17] In their eyes, the constitutional Act gave official status to the notion of Canada and contained in embryo the principle of responsible government which was flouted by the "Castle Clique"—the governer and his entourage.

With the threat of union out of the way, at least for the time being, Étienne Parent used his pamphlets to attack authoritarianism and disrespect for freedom of the press. As he was well aware of the liberal ideas of his age (particularly the "Whig" conception of the parliamentary system), the editor of *Le Canadien* sought merely the application of the fundamental principle of the British system, namely election, by an electoral body made up of enfranchised landowners (as in the British metropolis), of members of a legislative Council and governing responsibility for the Assembly which was also made up of members similarly elected by enfranchised propertyowners.[18] It is clear that before developing the deep fascination for the American economic example he was to speak of in his 1846–47 lectures, Parent was first influenced by British political liberalism. From 1823 to 1825, the young editor of *Le Canadien* was a tireless defender of these liberal principles, which led him to take a stand on several controversial issues, among them the problem of the seigneurial régime in Lower Canada and the struggles of the European and South American nationalist movements.[19] In each case, Étienne Parent measured the situation or problem against the yardstick of liberalism and condemned, sometimes most vehemently, the marks of feudalism.[20]

From 1825 to 1831, the principal journalistic organs for the Canadian, or Patriotic (from 1827), Party were *La Minerve*, founded in 1826 by Augustin–Norbert Morin, and the French section of the *Gazette de Québec*. In 1830, France was once again disturbed by the political changes that were to lead to the July Monarchy. These changes of régime had a great influence on French-Canadian patriots, because they established in France a moderate, liberal monarchy on the British model. The French-Canadian leaders hoped that a similar régime would be set up in the British colonies. Until 1834, the year of the presentation of the 92 Resolutions, many patriots were still constitutional monarchists, and it took Lord Russell's disappointing but logical response in 1837 to turn them into Republicans. Although he was critical of the decision made in London, Étienne Parent was not tempted to preach republicanism, despite his early fascination with the American economic example. Meanwhile, the French-Canadian liberals took up publication of *Le Canadien* again with the new issue appearing on 7 May 1831.

Étienne Parent was again named editor. He took on this task in addition to being librarian of the Assembly from 1833 to 1835. In this capacity, he presented two reports, published on 7 January 1834 and 27 October 1835, in which he argued for organizational reforms of the library and better accessibility.[21] In 1835, he became clerk of the Assembly.

Until 1838, Parent was more of a liberal democrat than a nationalist.[22] This feature of his thought and commitment is probably at the root of his differences with Louis-Joseph Papineau and the Montreal Patriots. The editor of *Le Canadien* was preaching moderation and patience just when the Montreal Patriots were preparing for insurrection. He went on supporting Governor Gosford, who made him a justice of the peace in 1836.[23] And when Governor Gosford made his first throne speech on 27 December 1835, Étienne Parent gave it a favorable review in *Le Canadien*.[24] In 1835–36, he campaigned tirelessly for the application of what was practised in England itself, namely responsible government.[25] He claimed that the colonies, especially Lower Canada, were capable of administering themselves and that they had attained the necessary level of maturity. Nonetheless, at the time when, as Gérard Bergeron puts it, "the first wind of a possible rebellion stirred in the Montreal region,"[26] Étienne Parent emphasized the advantages of a peaceful way and the fact that revolutionary views were "premature."[27] When Monseigneur Lartigue, Bishop of Montreal, gave his approval to strictly peaceful solutions, condemning the revolt against legitimate authority, Parent supported him.[28] During the summer of 1837, Étienne Parent's moderation was condemned by radicals who founded another journal, *Le Libéral* (published from June to November 1837), in order to counteract the views of *Le Canadien*.[29]

The process of revolt was underway. The first riots took place in Montreal on 7 November 1837. Parent left town, a move that was interpreted by government forces as an attempt to rally the countryside. Armed confrontations took place in Saint–Eustache, Saint–Denis and Saint–Charles. Several of the defeated insurgents took refuge in the United States. They were joined by William Mackenzie, leader of the rebels in Upper Canada who were also easily defeated.[30]

An enquiry was set up to investigate the causes of the conflict, and Great Britain sent out a special investigator, John Lambton, the first Lord Durham. Nicknamed "Radical Jack" when he played a major role in England's electoral reform of 1832, Lord Durham was a typical representative of the "Whig" aristocracy of the first third of the nineteenth century, aware of the need to create a space for the rising industrial middleclass, in order to maintain, paradoxically, aristocratic liberalism. Having been British ambassador to Russia, Durham accepted his posting to Canada without enthusiasm. "This is a doubly difficult task," he wrote, "and nothing but the extreme urgency of the situation could persuade me to make such a sacrifice."[31]

He arrived in Quebec in May 1838, flanked by Edward Gibbon Wakefield and Charles Buller, two reformists of the colonies. Durham realised very quickly that the conflict revolved basically around the question of responsible government. Étienne Parent eagerly welcomed the arrival of this new Governor General. Within the space of six months, Durham made a cool analysis of the situation and concluded that responsible government ought to be granted to the Assembly.

The principle could not be applied to Lower Canada, however, because that would place the Anglophone minority under the domination of Francophone authority. Consequently, it would be necessary to unite the two colonies, and to wait patiently until Anglophones were in the majority. Durham did not understand the opposition of the French-Canadian political leaders to the commercial and industrial projects of the Anglophone Montreal middle-class, and interpreted their obstruction as a refusal of economic change. The union of the two colonies seemed the ideal solution to a multidimensional problem in which, especially in Lower Canada, the struggle for responsible government was going on at the same time as the struggle within the same state between two nations, or two "races," as they were termed at the time.

After London refused amnesty to some of the resurgents in exile, as Durham had recommended, the latter hurried back to England to confront his opposition. His report was not published until February 1839, when it was printed in *The Times* of London. Étienne Parent hastened to translate it and published it in *Le Canadien* between 8 April and 8 May 1839.[32] The document, which filled more than 300 pages, was long debated.

In the meantime, a second rebellion took place in November of 1838, and for several days the area southwest of Montreal was controlled by the Patriots. In Napierville, there was even a declaration of independence. But the commander of the British troops, Sir John Colborne, quickly put down the rebellion. More than 900 insurgents were taken prisoner, 108 brought to trial, and 99 condemned to death. In the end, twelve were actually executed and fifty-eight were sent into exile.[33]

Étienne Parent severely criticized several of Durham's initiatives, particularly his naming of Adamton, an influential member of the "Montrealer" party, to important offices.[34] It also seemed more and more obvious that Durham was in favor of union of the two colonies. Parent, although still a pacifist, seems to have turned to the Patriots in his disillusionment with the special investigator.[35] When he denounced Colborne's arbitrary decisions, he was arrested on 26 December 1839; he was not released until 12 April 1839. On his release from prison, he immediately went on with the publication of the Durham report, which he had begun on 8 April. Although he was opposed to the union sanctioned by London in 1840, Parent endorsed the call for moderation made by Louis–Hippolyte Lafontaine (1807–1864), which was pub-lished in *Le Canadien*. The new leader of the French Canadians was recommending an alliance with the reformists of Upper Canada in order to counteract the damaging effects of union. This was, in fact the only chance of salvation for French Canadians. Étienne Parent was in favor of this strategy and was elected member of the Assembly of United Canada in 1841.[36] On 24 June 1842, he was the first orator invited to speak at the first ceremony of the Saint–Jean Baptiste Society in Quebec City. It should be remembered that it was Parent who had first suggested in 1834 the idea, taken up by Ludger Duvernay, of creating a French-Canadian Society. In 1842, Parent and Lafontaine introduced a bill to have French recognized in the chamber. Finally, in October 1842, Parent, who was going deaf as a result of the bad conditions during his imprisonment in 1839, accepted the position of clerk of the Executive Council. Thus, he left his political career and bade farewell to *Le Canadien*. From then on, his life became "nomadic," as he lived in Kingston, Montreal, Toronto, Quebec, and finally Ottawa.[37] As a high-ranking civil servant, he was at the centre of the process of the application of the principle of responsible government in 1848.

Besides being an editor, Étienne Parent began to study law in 1824. He articled with the firm of Charles–Eusèbe Casgrain and Joseph–Rémi Vallières in Saint–Réal. In 1825, he became editor of the French section of the *Gazette de Québec*, and having an enormous capacity for work, he accepted the post of translator in the Lower Canada Assembly in 1827. In the meantime, *Le Canadien* had to close its operation once more in 1825.[38]

In 1825, after being admitted to the Bar on 18 May, Parent married Marie–Mathilde–Henriette Grenier.[39] They had six children, five girls and a boy: Étienne–Henri (1835–1910), Joséphine–Henriette (1837–1926), Mathilde–Sabine (1838–?), Marie–Augustine (1841–1918), Marguerite (1832–34) and Stéphanie (1846–48). Joséphine–Henriette married the famous Antoine Gérin–Lajoie (1824–1882), and Marie–Augustine became the wife of another well-known personality, Benjamin Sulte (1841–1923).

THE FIRST LECTURES

Antoine Gérin–Lajoie made his mark on Canadian literature with the novels *Jean Rivard Le Défricheur* (1862) and *Jean*

Rivard L'Économiste (1864), a non-fiction text, *Dix ans d'his-toire du Canada,* and the lyrics to the song "Un Canadien errant."[40] As a young man, Gérin–Lajoie was fascinated by the United States and went there twice before marrying Joséphine–Henriette in 1858. From 1837 to 1844, Gérin–Lajoie had studied with the Abbé Ferland at the Collège de Nicolet. Ferland had introduced the young Gérin–Lajoie to the English language and Anglo-Saxon culture.[41] This was a decisive influence on Gérin–Lajoie's development, as he became infat-uated with liberal Anglo-Saxon (or Anglo-American) ideas.[42] As soon as he finished his studies, Gérin–Lajoie became one of the founders of the Canadian Institute and one of its main activists.[43] He was, successively, secretary-archivist, vice-presi-dent, president for three terms, and recording-secretary. It was during his presidency that Étienne Parent, who was not yet his father-in-law, gave his first lectures to the Canadian Institute in 1846 and 1847. They were on the following topics:

- Industry considered as a means of preserving our nationality (22 January 1846);

- The importance of studying political economy (19 November 1846);

- Of work and man (23 September 1847).

In these three lectures which dealt with a common subject, namely the post-Act of Union preservation of the French-Canadian nation, Étienne Parent set himself up as an unconditional defender of industry, study, and work. It was of prime importance, he stressed, that French Canadians should progress according to the Anglo-Saxon model, which he saw as middle-class and industrial. Parent had scant respect for the aristocratic prejudice against work, and was an avowed and unqualified admirer of what he perceived, already at this time, as the Anglo-American model, which would guarantee the future of a nation through work, trade, and industry.

Right at the moment Étienne Parent was writing, Great Britain was preparing to adopt free trade and to abandon its protectionist political economy. These were changes prompted by the Industrial Revolution, which had developed slowly in the cotton industry throughout the eighteenth century before transforming other branches of the textile, transport and iron and steel industry from 1820 to 1850.[44] Even if France was not associated with the Industrial Revolution in the first half of the nineteenth century, it had, nevertheless, undergone major transformations and had seen its economy develop at the same rate as British growth between 1815 and 1850.[45] It was not until 1850 to 1870 that Great Britain broke away completely.[46] As for the American Industrial Revolution, it did not come into its stride until the second half of the nineteenth century. The view Étienne Parent expressed in 1846, of a pre-Revolutionary France and a capitalist Great Britain, already underestimated the development of capitalism in France and overestimated the phenomenon of the Industrial Revolution in England itself, not to mention the United States.

This said, what Parent did do in his first lecture was give a definition of industry as "manual labor guided by intelligence." French Canada should encourage industry and commerce, and above all ensure "the survival, from one generation to another, of commercial [and other] enterprises." Furthermore, for Parent, agriculture should not be seen as a bulwark against industrialization, but rather as a complementary sector. If French Canada did not take precautionary measures, the lecturer warned, it would be completely swallowed up by the Anglo-Saxon world. Étienne Parent was haunted by this spectre. Hence his insistence on identifying industry as "the only source of wealth" and as "the only means of acquiring social importance."

In the second lecture, given on 19 November 1846 and entitled "The importance of the study of political economy," Parent again expressed his enthusiasm for the Anglo-American world, but once again, also, his fear of the economic and social marginalisation of French Canadians. At the end of 1846, it looked more and more likely that unified Canada would get responsible government in compensation for Great Britain's abandonment of protectionism. French Canadians should, according to Parent, from now on concentrate on the economic struggle. There again, as the political battle was not yet won, Étienne Parent had foreseen quite accurately the importance and significance of the changes in the political economy of Great Britain. French Canadians should give up "frivolous" reading and devote themselves to "useful and instructive" reading of classic authors of political economy. Parent himself had an excellent knowledge of the texts of Adam Smith (1723–1740), François Quesnay (1694–1774), and Jean–Baptiste Say (1767–1832), and complete disdain for the "French columnists," especially Alexandre Dumas and Eugène Sue. Parent's point seems to have been taken. Professor Yvan Lamonde[47] has shown that the Canadian Institute library, although well-stocked with the works of classic economists, was overflowing with works of "columnists," who explicated, sometimes extraordinarily lucidly, the social problems of their day. Parent's judgement was overly severe. Besides making reference to classic authors like Adam Smith, Edmund Burke, the Abbé de Saint–Pierre, and Jean–Baptiste Say, the lecturer showed a lively interest in important contemporary events, particularly in this passage: "if something is going to come of the realization of the dream we call the dream of the decent man, it will be universal free trade; and Sir Robert Peel's Cereals Act is the first step in this direction...."

Other passages of this lecture could also apply to present-day debates about the economy and state expense. Taking the example of an act supposedly "for the protection of agriculture," Étienne Parent is at pains to show that "protection is a ridiculous and disastrous system, except, perhaps in a few specific cases where the initial stages of a new industry have to be supported.... or where the failure of an old industry has to be off-set...."

The lecturer ended by pointing out with great pride the fact that the Collège de Saint–Hyacinthe had put courses on the elements of political economy on its syllabus. Much taken by this initiative, Étienne Parent added, "a few hundred louis a year over a few years for chairs in political economy, will save the province hundreds of thousands of louis, either in losses avoided or in gains through economic understanding." At his conclusion, he launched into a stirring appeal to the country, and a veritable panegyric of work as the supreme value bringing humanity closer to God.

Work was also the central theme of the third lecture, given on 23 September 1847. In this lecture, Parent expressed unambiguously his fascination and admiration for the United States. In the first part of the lecture, he criticized those who were disdainful of work, and declared straight out that Anglo-Americans valued work more than French Canadians. A person who did not value work, in the eyes of this liberal thinker, was "guilty of resisting the will of the Creator." Some of the formulae and expressions used by Parent in this text are religiously inspired. For example: "the most industrious people are almost always the people who enjoy the greatest freedom..."; and "the absurd idea, which is insulting to the Divinity, as well as being pernicious to humanity, according to which work is a sentence to which man has been condemned by the Creator." On the contrary, for Parent, work is "the continuation of the creative task of God."

In the second part of this speech, Étienne Parent went so far as to claim that the United States (or America) was fulfilling the will of God. "But America joined forces with its young and vigorous populations one day to reveal another God to the world, a God of free men, a God of the workers." Parent certainly wielded considerable influence over the members of the Canadian Institute. His talks, given ten years after the rebellions of 1837–38, announced the moderate, pragmatic liberalism that characterized French-Canadian liberals in the nineteenth and even the twentieth century. It must be emphasized that this liberalism, under Parent's pen, was profoundly coloured by admiration for the Anglo-American model: "The English work like artists, for the love of work itself"; or, as he elaborates elsewhere, "the Anglo-Saxon industrial worker, whether he is a craftsman or an agricultural laborer, hopes, though his art or his skill, to advance, to rise in the social scale, and with this aim in mind, he is constantly seeking ways or means to make his work more efficient and more perfect, and more often than not, he succeeds."

Parent wages a tireless battle against slothfulness: "through work alone is man king of creation.... And whoever does not contribute to this work of divine destiny to the full extent of his faculties resists divine will..., renounces his birthright and the supremacy granted to man over all creation and debases himself till he is at the level of brutish and inert nature."

Fascinated by the Protestant ethic, Parent gives this advice to wealthy French Canadians:

Develop your wealth, increase your fortune: the accumulation of capital gives birth to great enterprises—work. You don't feel you have any talent for business, devote yourself to some useful study, enrich your mind—work. If you do not have the wherewithal for intellectual work, do some charitable task: everyone can do his neighbor a good turn. That is also work, and not the least worth-while work.... The riches you lavish on luxury objects and frivolous amusements should not concern you; they would have existed without you.... Give back to society what you owe it, to God what He expects of you in the great task of progress and the happiness of mankind.

It is difficult for us today to imagine the importance of these lectures. The press of the day, which published these texts, made them into major events by simply reproducing the texts.[48] Until 1848, the Canadian Institute had its quarters in 25, rue Saint–Gabriel; in 1850–51, the Institute moved to the Oddfellows Hall in the Grande rue Saint–Jacques; finally, from 1854 to 1864 they were in the rue Notre–Dame, then rue Sainte–Thérèse, then back to rue Notre–Dame from 1866. Montreal had 57,715 inhabitants in 1852 and 90,323 in 1861. One can imagine the effervescence surrounding the Canadian Institute at least until 1869, the year it was closed by Monseigneur Bourget. But the thinking of Étienne Parent remained influential long after the closing down of the Institute (Couture, 1991). Besides, the lectures enjoyed an unequivocal success. Some lectures attracted between 700 and 800 people; Parent's probably had an audience of several hundred. Yvan Lamonde (1990) writes that, at that time, for lectures, an average of 200 people was a reasonable figure. In 1848, Étienne Parent brought two other themes to members and friends of the Montreal Institute.

It was in the context of the acquisition of responsible government that Étienne Parent gave his fourth lecture, some five months after the last. As Gérard Bergeron insists, this lecture was probably the most symmetrical in construction.[49] The author first laid out his theme, in this case, education, which he defined thus: "the perfecting of all the attributes possessed by man in society. Thus, education is, at the same time, moral and religious, physical and intellectual." He went on to identify four "flaws" in the education system which have four corresponding solutions.[50]

Flaws

1. Independent or exclusive administration of school business by elected boards.

2. Proportional tax on property, distributed and designated by the same boards.

3. Sufficient compensation for institutions not guaranteed.

4. Obligation by each district, without exception, to contribute an equal amount to the legislative allocation.

Solutions

1. Supreme central administration with the assistance of local boards in nominating members of the central authority.

2. Scaled property taxes set by legislation and distributed and prioritized by the executive.

3. Amounts received by institutions set by law.

4. Partial or complete exemption for poor areas from contributing an equal amount to the legislative allocation.

As a background to these solutions, Parent defended the thesis that reform of the education system was urgent and important for French Canada: "the question of education is a vital, pressing one for our people; we must have education at any cost, by any means and not a moment must be lost...." All too aware of the situation of a French culture embedded in a British setting, he explicated in this lecture a policy of amalgamation of the two cultures and an elaboration of a pragmatic idealism:

In France, the saying goes: "Do your duty, come what may"; it's chivalrous, it's splendid. What I prefer for the majority of people, however, is the English adage: "Honesty is the best policy"; it's more tangible, more useful, better adapted to human nature. It's said that proverbs are the wisdom of nations; is it not true that the two I have just quoted give an accurate assessment of the character of the two nations to whom they belong?

Hence the programme laid out by Parent which was designed to support French Canada, specifically in the improvement of the education system: "Observe, on the other hand, the absolute supremacy of the press; surrounded by states much more powerful than itself, it felt that it should increase the strength of its people...: what did it do? It established a system of popular teaching...which serves as a model to the whole of the civilized world."

Since Locke, and, in the eighteenth century, Edmund Burke, the aristocratic liberal tradition, while making a distinction between a spiritual and a temporal dimension, is characterized by close ties between the divine and the economic, political, and social order. The natural evolution of societies, in the way it is explicitly described by Burke, is the work of God. Étienne Parent, who once again in this lecture displays a good knowledge of the classics (he quotes Plato as well as Rousseau, Lamartine, Guizot, and Machiavelli, and refers implicitly to Locke, Condorcet, Montesquieu, Helvétius, Diderot, Say, etc.), in fact expressed in all his lectures a rigorous, classic liberal vision founded on a balance between the spiritual dimension and political and economic necessity.

There was, then, a certain logic in the fact that Étienne Parent, after proposing reforms in the area of education and setting down the fundamental principles, took up in the fifth lecture given to the Canadian Institute on 17 December 1848, the theme of the place "of the priest and of spirituality and their relationship with society."

At first, the lecturer defined spirituality as all "that affects the human soul, its feelings, its aspirations, its needs, as opposed to what, in men, effects the senses, the desires, the affections, and also the needs—what I would call materialism." The priest is "spirituality personified."

These two forces, spirituality and materialism, enter into opposition if they are expressed in an extreme way. Hence, if you push spirituality too far, Parent wrote, "you will have a state in which the individual will be offered up as a burnt offering to the dominant idea, be that good or bad." On the other hand, "individualism which has become out of hand is destructive on account of its excessive concentration or isolation." The place of the priest is at the heart of the balance we must seek. Hence Parent's suggestion that priests should be more seriously encouraged to play a role of spiritual action in society and to fill certain lacunae, particularly the fact "that the education of priests has been seriously lacking in the area of public morals and political science."

Later in the lecture, he referred to the situation in revolutionary France in 1848 (the revolution broke out in February); he recalled the drama of the premier priest of France, Monseigneur Affre, Bishop of Paris, who perished as he tried to play the role of intermediary. It is clear that for Étienne Parent, the priest had the obligation to embody the moral fibre of the nation, of the country, and to watch out for abuse committed in the name of opulence. Capitalistic progress must encourage increased wealth without ostentation. Thus, "the church must be the soul, the reason of society, the state its body, its senses." Each sphere has a complementary but distinct role. The priest, however, should not be contemplative

in the century in which we live; I, at least could not understand the existence of communities of men devoted to the purely contemplative life in a hair shirt and sackcloth; in my view it would constitute a deplorable aberration of spirituality. I would say the same of all religious practices that tend to weaken man's sense of independence, of the self-reliance of the English or that reduce God and man at the same time if they are substituted for the active, male virtues that society needs.

In short, Étienne Parent was proposing to the Catholic Church a *modus vivendi* that would allow it to play an essential role in modern economic development in the nineteenth century, such as the lecturer had analyzed in his first series of lectures. This vision of a society going busily about its tasks, morally balanced even during an Industrial Revolution, would be even better articulated in the last series of lectures.

THE LAST LECTURES

In his capacity as clerk of the executive council, from 1842 on, Étienne Parent was constantly travelling. This explains, perhaps, the fact that he took on the last series of lectures in 1848. Starting in this year, united Canada experienced a series of important events, among them the annexation manifesto in 1849, the abolition of the seigneurial régime, the treaty of commercial reciprocity with the United States in 1854, negotiations with a view to forming a confederation in 1864, and finally the new régime inaugurated in 1867. Given his position, Étienne Parent could not comment on events as he had as editor of *Le Canadien*; the last lectures, however, thanks to their extraordinary foresight and to the sense of anticipation that Parent generated, gave an almost premonitory interpretation to each of these events.

The last lectures were delivered in Quebec City. The first was organized by the "Society for early closing of stores" and was given on 15 January 1852. The lectures of 22 January and 7 February were at the invitation of members of the Canadian Institute of Quebec, one of whose most active members was François–Xavier Garneau.[51] And the last lecture, on 15 April 1852, attracted not only members of the public but particularly members of the Reading Circle of Saint–Roch, who had invited the famous lecturer.

As an introduction to the conference given in Quebec City, Étienne Parent defined the nature of his audience when he wrote, "I feel I should act as interpreter between you and your bosses, who, with intentions as liberal as they are patriotic, have allowed you to devote your long evenings to our instruction." Apparently, the audience consisted mainly of young men, "shop assistants who were finishing their education," as Gérard Bergeron puts it.[52] The thesis Étienne Parent was defending that evening was the same one he had defended in 1846 and 1847, namely that commerce is the essential element by which French Canada could raise itself. The lecturer gave as examples the success of ten or so French-Canadian enterprises that were at the head of several Canadian commercial branches, among them those of Thibodeau and Chinic, and of the poet Octave Crémazie and his father Joseph Crémazie, both owners of a bookstore which was a meeting place for Quebec intellectuals. As was his tendency, Étienne Parent urged his listeners to follow the example of French Canadians who were involved in business. Then he launched into a condensed version of the history of world trade from the Phoenicians to Christopher Columbus. It is extremely interesting to note that Parent, along with many American intellectuals of the late eighteenth and early nineteenth centuries was a great admirer of the commercial cities of the Mediterranean, particularly Carthage and Rome (later medieval Venice and Genoa).[53] The lecturer went on enthusiastically, "the discovery of America, gentlemen, is the greatest event of the modern era...and it is certainly and incontestably to trade that we owe it." Besides, without trade, "Quebec would still be Stadacona and Montreal Hochelaga...." Trade also brought about technical progress, symbolized by the railroads that crossed "our primitive forests" and by the steamboat.

Parent was so fascinated by trade and "progress" that he waxed lyrical about it: "trade is, after the Christian religion, the most important instrument in the hands of God, for the moral and intellectual advancement of mankind, since it puts into contact civilization and barbarity, or states with a more advanced civilization with those which are less so."

Further on in the lecture, Étienne Parent again brought up his enthusiasm for political economy and economic liberalism. "Beautiful dreams have been built and are still being built on human brotherhood, on ways of achieving universal fraternity. The safest of these ways is in trade and in free trade." And again, "it is because of its lack of commercial and industrial genius that Spain foundered, whereas it is through the possession of these qualities that England prospered."

Although a theoretical free-trader, the lecturer was still aware of the stakes involved in international competition and argued for a circumstantial and moderate protectionism. He wrote, "As a free-trader, I am in principle opposed as much to production subsidies as to protectionist rights. But I am not one of those who say: 'Preserve your country rather than a principle.' I say: let us preserve our country with our principles intact if we can, but with modified principles, if necessary." Parent was fearful for the situation of a "young country which lacks experience and capital" and made a plea for a national commercial and industrial development that would allow free trade that was equitable for all.

On the question of the development of a national industry, Étienne Parent was proud to mention the example of Monsieur Charles Têtu, an industrialist from the River Ouelle, who had had a certain success at his booth at the Great Exhibition of Industry in London in 1851 with his "porpoise leather cured by himself." On the other hand, this example showed the importance of protecting Canadian territorial waters so that national fishermen and industrialists could succeed.

Later, still in the name of economic liberal rationalism, Étienne Parent revealed once again his opposition to the seigneurial régime, which he described as a "formidable obstacle to industry, to the establishment of domestic factories" (he had previously condemned the seigneurial régime in the 1820s). Apart from a few exceptional seigneuries, like the one at Terrebonne and the one belonging to the seminary of Quebec, where there were mills, foundries, or factories, "the seigneurs have no thought but to increase their own property." Étienne Parent's wish came true in 1854 with the abolition of the seigneurial tenure.

The other major obstacle to the realization of a commercial and industrial revolution in French Canada was the inadequacy of the educational system. For Étienne Parent, it was essential to adapt education to the new realities and to prevent the perpetuation of a system in which "up until now, commercial and industrial education has been more or less non-existent." The lecture ended with a stirring call to youth, with an extraordinarily prescient passage about the future development of the west and the formation of modern Canada: "Towards the west, we have an immense country which will soon be the granary of the world, and for which our Saint Lawrence is the natural highway to the sea."

In short, in this lecture which appeared so harmless, Étienne Parent touched on all the major issues of his time and sketched the political and economic future of Canada. Although aware of the danger of assimilation with the United States (he must have been very concerned over the subject of the annexionist manifesto), he nonetheless expressed his unfailing admiration for the American economic model. A proponent of free-trade, he understood the importance of protecting, for a while, at least, national trade which encouraged economic "progress." He understood the urgency of abolishing the seigneurial system and reforming the education system; as a visionary, he already had an intimation of the development of the Canadian west. Such was Étienne Parent, remarkable for the fusion he wrought between liberalism, economic and political, on the one hand, and nationalism on the other.

ON INTELLIGENCE AND ITS RELATIONSHIP TO SOCIETY

In the opinion of several commentators, this lecture, which was given in two parts, on 22 January and 7 February 1852, for the members of the Canadian Institute of Quebec, was the most important given by Étienne Parent. It took up a theme already tackled in "Considerations on our public education, on education in general and on the legislative means to achieve it" (1848). And as in that 1848 lecture, he divided his analysis into eight main sections relating to a reform in the education system.

In his introductory remarks, Étienne Parent emphasized the importance he placed on the separation between Church and State which should form "two distinct and separate forces." Intelligence should be applied sometimes to "spiritual things" and sometimes to "temporal things." Further on, he says, "by intelligence...I mean, in the context at hand, the power of conception, aptitude and energy which makes possible great things in all areas of human activity, with the exception of the question of morality, which, according to my theory, falls into the domain of spiritual power."

Before turning to his eight proposals, Étienne Parent analyzed the big political questions of his time. He first gave a justification for the idea of "utopian government of the masses" and also, despite his obvious respect for the individual, for the socialist projects of Louis Blanc, evoking the events of 1848 to 1851 in France. On the other hand, he condemned equally vehemently "hereditary government" and especially slavery as being "an abomination in the sight of God and man." Parent, who execrated the Revolution of 1789 and all revolutionary measures, proposed the following plan to ensure that social change should occur naturally:

> To achieve this goal, I do not propose overturning the social and political arrangements that already exist; my plan could be accommodated to any régime. You are in favor of a monarchy?—my plan would not gainsay you, for it is within the monarchy that I found my source of inspiration, my initial idea. You are in favor of democracy?—my plan fits perfectly; popular election suits it better than court patronage. You are in favor of the aristocratic principle? Aha! It's a true aristocracy that I'm offering you, an aristocracy of intelligence, which is better, is it not? than the aristocracy of the sword, or of parchment or of the stock exchange. But to be more precise. If I had to convert my plan into a proposal for an act of law, here are the title and the main points of an act to ensure the development and enhancement of intelligence:

1. Free, primary education for all children.

2. Free education at higher levels for all those deemed deserving of it by their talents and good behavior.

3. Grants will be given to needy children who have to leave home to continue their education.

4. In order to occupy any executive, legislative, judiciary, municipal public office a certain level of educational attainment must be reached, depending on the importance or the nature of the office.

5. Advance loans, with or without interest, to needy students in post-secondary education, who do not have

paid, public employment, but who wish to gain qualification for entry into a profession or the arts or industry.

6. Diplomas testifying to the levels they have achieved will be granted to students who have satisfied public and solemn examination; those who have such diplomas will form an élite society called "the Educated Class" which will enjoy the rights and privileges mentioned above and any others society decides to bestow on them.

6. A central office will be created at certain times to supervise the execution of this law, initially through executive power, and later by a body composed of members of the educated class, with the right to delegate its powers to local offices or to peripatetic agents in remote areas of the country. Wide disciplinary powers will be granted to this office.[54]

7. Special funding shall be created for this Act through a progressive tax on wills, inheritance and gifts or donations; in case of fraud, these will be subject to confiscation, with the money going to the fund.

The lecturer finished his talk on this eighth point. He promised his listeners to elaborate on the plan in the next lecture.

ON INTELLIGENCE AND ITS RELATIONSHIP WITH SOCIETY: PART TWO

Étienne Parent did indeed elaborate his plans in the lecture given on 7 February, as we have already mentioned. The principle he was defending was quite simple: the state should be responsible for primary education of all children. After that, everything would depend on merit and talent. This is contained in his first three points. The fourth aimed at making advancement in public office dependent on merit. The fifth principle, as the reader will have seen, anticipated a system of loans for "needy" students. Articles 7 and 8 (or the second 6 and 7) took on the question of administration, through the creation of a central office, and the financing, through the creation of a special fund, this plan of developing intelligence. As for article 6 (the first one), it called for the recognition of an educated élite which would come out of this system.

This plan makes fascinating reading, as it contains several measures that would be proposed a century later in the famous "Parent Report" (Monseigneur Alphonse–Henri Parent) on education in Quebec. The last part is also prophetic, as the author brings up, albeit in a paternalistic way, the place of women in this system: "Barbarism has always enslaved women, civilization emancipates them." In particular, Étienne Parent took an interest in the "daughters of the people," but recommended patience to them in a tone imbued with paternalism: "there is much to be done for the daughter of the people; but she must be patient; she must wait until her brothers have themselves achieved their place in society. Then they will take her by the hand and raise her to their level...."

Thus Étienne Parent ended his second lecture on intelligence by bringing out another aspect of French-Canadian society, in this case the place of women, which became, in the twentieth century, an essential political question. It remained to the lecturer to expound on another reality, still embryonic in the middle of the nineteenth century, but one that would become fundamental with the growing importance of the Industrial Revolution: the question of the working class.

CONSIDERATIONS ON THE FATE OF THE WORKING CLASSES

This theme had been broached on 15 April 1852 at the Reading Circle of Saint–Roch, a working-class district of the capital, since Quebec had once again become, for a while (four years) the seat of government.

As in his first lectures of 1846 to 1847, Étienne Parent made a connection between God, Providence, and economic laws. Once again he rejected any revolutionary project and urged the workers to accept their fate. "God who made man a social being, so that the whole of humanity should form a single, collective whole, gave an unequal and disparate share of intelligence, aptitudes and tastes to men and thus He assigned to every man his place." Besides, economic laws "like all other laws of nature, are independent of man and were ordained by the Creator for the government of the social world, and there is no way they can be changed...." And again, "The cost of work, like everything else associated with commerce, is calculated by competition...." The worker cannot, therefore, change his salary artificially. However, in order to protect workers from the vagaries of the economy, and sometimes, from the abuse of some bosses, Étienne Parent proposed the creation of compulsory savings-banks into which owners would have to deposit a certain fixed dowry sum. In addition, workers in the same occupation could form groups "to find work in other places if there was none where they were." The lecture ended with a long diatribe against Father Chiquiny, formerly praised in the 1848 lecture on spiritualism, who had left Quebec to found a religious sect in the United States. Étienne Parent strongly disapproved of the American exile of numbers of French Canadians and wanted to set up colonization funds to allow unemployed workers to remain in the country, as in Upper Canada where the unemployed were made to work on road construction. Once again, the reader is fascinated by the fact that this theme of colonization as a cure for unemployment became current during the first third of the twentieth century as much in French Canada in the rest of the Anglo-American world, particularly during the economic crisis of the 1930s (Garraty, 1987).

THE CIVIL SERVICE AND FEDERALISM

This lecture on the working class was the last given by Étienne Parent, at least in his capacity as "lecturer." In 1859, in the *Journal de l'instruction publique*, he published an article on Pierre Bédard and his two sons. Parent still felt a great affection for the founder of *Le Canadien*. This affection was also ideological in the sense that through Bédard, the former director of *Le Canadien,* rediscovered his passion for British political liberalism which he had never renounced, despite his commitment to the American economic model.

In the 1850, famous French author Edmé de Saint–Père visited Canada and in 1859 published *La France aux Colonies*; Étienne Parent kept up a correspondence with him for about ten years. Jean–Charles Falardeau has written of this correspondence, without, however giving any references, that "Parent used these long letters as a pretext for recalling the outline of the history of the country, for commenting on events such as the Fenian raids or the American Civil War or the benefits that Canadian federation would bring."[55] On the question of slavery, Étienne Parent had already expressed his indignation in the lectures on "intelligence" in 1852. As for his position on the American conflict, it is reasonable to imagine that, with his preference for an industrial society and against aristocratic domination, he supported the North and its anti-slavery and industrial position.

With respect to Confederation, he was able to express his unwavering support during a ceremony at Rimouski in 1868 in the presence of Georges–Étienne Cartier: "I do not flinch to proclaim, gentlemen, that in my opinion Canadian Confederation is one of those providential events of which our history offers several examples."[56] And later he said,

> And if someone here were tempted to accuse me of being a proponent after the fact, or a latter day federalist, allow me to refer him to *Le Canadien* going back to the month of July 1838, exactly thirty years ago next July. If that doesn't give me the right to be called a forerunner of federalism or even a proto-forerunner, then by heaven, no-one else has that right. I think I must have been the first French Canadian who dared to speak his mind publicly in favor of Confederation as being the safest way of saving our nationality, in that it would free us from all foreign interference in our national institutions by handing them over completely to our safe keeping though our local legislation. And my reasons are still valid today.[57]

For people of Parent's generation, 1867 was a political victory, for the British North America Act gave back part of the virtual sovereignty contained in the Constitutional Act of 1791. The creation of provinces able to pass laws on education and the recognition of French in Article 133 of the British North America Act constituted important political victories. Ideological architect of the BNA Act, Étienne Parent was named under-secretary of state in the federal government in 1868. He served until 1872 and died in 1874.

At the beginning of this chapter, we pointed out that Étienne Parent appears unknown today. Parent, indeed, never enjoyed the fame of a Louis–Joseph Papineau. He was, nonetheless, the discrete but profoundly influential architect of the reformist compromise of the 1840s, and the undisputed theoretical master of one, if not several, generations of French-Canadian moderate liberals. Yet he seems to have been the object of periodic homage and at least of obligatory reference.

As early as 1874, Hector Fabre (1834–1910), who later became Canada's representative in Paris, marked in *L'Événement* the sad passing of the great intellectual leader who was "one of us, but greater than us."[58] Three years later, Wilfrid Laurier proposed a moderate definition of liberalism that repeated the broad outline of the political and economic liberalism of the former director of *Le Canadien*.[59] It should also be noted that the liberals of Honoré Mercier's National Party, founded in 1885, belonged very obviously to the same liberal current. Among the founders were Louis–Amable Jetté, former lawyer for the Notre–Dame factory in the Guibord affair; Frédéric–Liguori Béique, a lawyer who became influential initially in the government of Honoré Mercier, and later under Wilfrid Laurier at the federal level; Laurent–Olivier David, future biographer of Laurier; Côme–Séraphon Chevrier; Josephe Doutre; Félix–Gabriel Marchand; Honoré Mercier, of course; and Wilfrid Laurier himself.[60] This generation exerted a determining influence on Canada through the two last decades of the nineteenth century and the beginning of the twentieth. Even after 1919, the year of Laurier's death, moderate liberals like Frédéric–Liguori Béique and Raoul Dandurand continued to wield a profound influence on the Canadian economic and political world.[61]

The intellectual presence of Étienne Parent throughout this period was symbolized by the re-edition of James Huston's *Répertoire national* in 1893 and by his flattering presentation of the journalist, civil servant, and lecturer.[62] Particularly stressed was the prophetic nature of a lecture like "On intelligence and its relationship with society" given in 1852, some two years after the publication of the fourth volume of the *Répertoire national*, containing Parent's first five lectures. "Here is a work worthy of meditation by philosophical thinkers," it said, "and whose value and importance we will only understand later, when study and political experience are more advanced among us."[63] Some ten years later, the publication by Gérard Malchelosse of the *Mélanges historiques* by Benjamin Sulte, Parent's son-in-law, perpetuated, especially in Sulte's writing, the mythological nature of the man.[64] Volume fourteen of these *Mélanges* was republished in 1928 by Édouard Garant;[65] in 1936, Gérard Parizeau published "Mon ami Étienne Parent."[66] A few years later, in 1939, Monseigneur Camille Roy presented the moderate liberal thinker in a favorable light, describing him, in *Manuel d'histoire de la littérature canadienne de langue française*, as an important author.[67] Monseigneur Émile Chartier said of the great journalist in 1941 "that he was a sentinel keeping watch on the heights...."[68] The post-war period was also a propitious time for the "rediscovery" of Parent, with publications by Paul–Eugène Gosselin[69] and François–Albert Angers,[70] Arthur Saint–Pierre,[71] and Mason Wade.[72] Even the years 1960 and 1970 were not exempt from studies—remarkable studies, but unfortunately not sufficiently known—on Étienne Parent. Brief mention should be made of the works of Louis Nourry,[73] Benoît Bernier,[74] Urbain Blanchet,[75] and Jean–Charles Falardeau.[76] Recently, Étienne Parent was again the object of fascination, particularly in the works of Gérard Bergeron, Gilles Gallichan,[77] Claude

Doyon,[78] and Stéphane Kelly.[79] In an intellectually challenging book published in 1997, Kelly argued that Étienne Parent was a "parvenu," or upstart, because he accepted the Constitution of 1867. According to Kelly, Parent had already expressed, in texts published in the late 1830s, his intention to "collaborate." But Parent never abandoned the concept of self-government for French Canada. Like Trudeau, Parent admired the Anglo-American world. But, contrary to Trudeau, he also thought that economic development based on private property was a universal reality that French Canadians, as individuals and as a collectivity, could promote. Then who is an upstart? The one who acknowledged a possible connection between liberalism and nationalism inside the French Canadian society, or the one who defined collectively the French Canadian society as monolithic and globally opposed to liberalism and individualism, which are supposed to be strictly Anglo-American?

As a matter of fact, one of the first authors to use the expression "ideological monolithism" was Pierre Elliott Trudeau.[80] Étienne Parent's name was rapidly brought up in Trudeau's text which deals mainly, as we have seen, with the French Canadian's "nationalism" that was in combat with liberalism.[81] But it is clear that the former editor of *Cité libre*, and many authors after him, was unable to think of the importance of the relation, obvious in Étienne Parent's texts, between classic liberalism (both élitist and aristocratic: socially conservative but progressive on the economic front) and French- Canadian nationalism of the years from 1850 to 1950. Not that the star lecturer of the Canadian Institute initiated the thought, or that he was some kind of absolute point of origin. But the profound lucidity with which he approached the social end economic context of his age, and which Parent expressed in the texts of his lectures in the middle of the nineteenth century (apart from the fact that he has appealed to several generations), challenges French Canada and Quebec at the end of the twentieth century. In this era of global trade and of Quebec's enthusiasm—and everyone else's—for private enterprise, Étienne Parent's lectures are compellingly up-to-date, despite the relative obscurity to which this important figure has been relegated.

NATIONALISM AND LIBERALISM

In the nineteenth century, the debate about nationalism mainly opposed those who accepted Herder's paradigm, developed in the eighteenth century, of the importance of language as a fundamental characteristic of a community and eventually a nation to those, on the contrary, who saw the individual, not a collectivity using a specific language, as the fundamental reality of a society. In the twentieth century, after the Second World War, the debate about nationalism reproduced the same fundamental division through different schools of thought.

On one hand, advocates of the nation-state building approach (Gellner, 1964; Greenfeld, 1992; Smith, 1983) saw in the tension between tradition and modernity resulting from modernization the source of nationalism. On the other hand, primordialists (Geertz, 1963) refused to limit the notion of nation to modern times and insisted on primordial factors anterior to modernity. Finally, writers like Elie Kedourie, who, according to Guy Laforest (1993), had a great deal of influence on Trudeau, dismissed nationalism as a foolish emanation of European romanticism.

In any case, the concept of modernization, the idea of a clash between tradition and modernity, is essential to the theorists of nationalism. But we have already expressed a certain skepticism, in chapter two, about the idea of modernization and the principle that tradition and modernity necessarily clashed in the nineteenth century. Étienne Parent, as we have established, is a perfect example of an individual coming from a so-called collectivist culture and society who was able to construct a vision, as early as 1848, in which the themes of economic development and industrialization were considered as universal and not limited to the Anglo-American world.

Étienne Parent, as we have seen, was a partisan of British political liberalism and of economic liberalism: he never believed in violence, even in 1837–38 when England deeply disappointed him by its refusal to grant the principle of responsible government. Although the American economic example had great appeal for him, he always understood the need to preserve the economic and political autonomy of Canada vis-à-vis the United States; much taken with political economy (Smith and Say are quoted in almost every one of his lectures), he was lucid enough to recognize that Canada would have to protect its national trade before it could countenance free trade.

In his essay on liberalism, André Vachet[82] identified the principal theses (liberty, security, equality, and property) and the principal themes (rationalism, naturalism, and individualism) of liberalism. The configuration of one form of liberalism as opposed to another depends on the difference in hierarchy in the links between these ideas and themes. Thus, so-called classic liberalism gives priority to the link between property and individualism. Is this form of liberalism incompatible with nationalism and religion? In England and the United States, possessive, individualist liberalism has been a fundamental ingredient of national identity.[83] By bringing about a fusion between economic political liberalism and French-Canadian nationalism, Étienne Parent did display an obvious admiration for the Anglo-American world, but he also expressed a strategy based on the following principle: since the essential ideas of political/ economic liberalism have universal application, French Canadians were perfectly able to appeal to it to advance their nationality, as did the Anglo-Americans. Now in England and the United States, this form of liberalism was always deeply religious. It still is, in fact. Need we remind ourselves, as did Macpherson,[84] of the importance of religion in Burke's liberalism, or as did Taylor[85] of its importance for Locke? This dimension is identical for Étienne Parent, who separates church and state, but who gives an essential place to Catholicism in an otherwise economically and politically autonomous society.

Since Pierre Elliott Trudeau's 1956 text and the no less famous Quiet Revolution, a malaise seems to have spread: the inability to grasp the complexity of the relationship between tradition and modernity in liberal thought; the classic French-Canadian liberals of the years 1850–1950 and even Duplessis himself, were, among others, its victims (Bourque, Duchastel, and Beauchemin, 1994). Whereas Étienne Parent was able to think of a certain form of liberalism within French Canada itself as a legitimate strategy, Pierre Elliott Trudeau and others after him have had their vision clouded by the image of a French Canada, in essence resistant to any form of liberalism, that was often pictured in Anglo-American intellectual circles. And is this inability to think of the relationship between classic liberalism and the nation other than in an Anglo-American context not, when all is said and done, the final result of a deep political colonialism?

the just society

individual rights and
collective rights

ONCE IN POWER, did Pierre Elliott Trudeau reproduce
the same ambiguities we have observed in his representation
of French-Canadian nationalist "monolithism"? In order to
answer that question, we should first look at Trudeau's definition of a "just society."

THE JUST SOCIETY

In *The Trudeau Years*, the former editor of *Cité libre* gives
this definition of the just society:

At a time like this, what attracted me to politics was no
longer the desire to fight for liberty, since that battle already
belonged to the past. In my mind, the value to put to the
fore in the pursuit of a just society was rather equality. Not a
Procustian equality, naturally, in which everyone would be
reduced to some common denominator. But equality of
opportunity.... Now Canada seems to me a land blessed by
the gods to pursue a policy of the greatest equality of opportunity. A young country, a rich country, a country with two
languages, a pluralist country with its ethnicities and its

religions, an immense country with varied geographic regions, a federalist country, Canada had, besides, a political tradition that was neither completely libertarian nor completely state dominated, but was based, rather, on the collaboration necessary between government and the private sector and on direct action of the State to protect the weak against the strong, the needy against the wealthy.[1]

The aim of a just society was to ensure equality of economic opportunity through aid to the regions and through recognition of the equality of French and English. In fact the Official Languages Act was the first attempt to try to entrench the principle of a just society.

THE OFFICIAL LANGUAGES ACT

The language question has obviously recurred constantly in Canadian history. As early as 1839, in his famous report, Lord Durham had reached the conclusion that the co-habitation of two linguistic groups in the same state was impossible. Thus, in the Act of Union of 1840, Article 41 stipulates the use of English only in the legislature. The victory of the Lafontaine-Baldwin reformists and the accomplishment of responsible government in 1848 were two factors that led to the repeal of this article and the subsequent recognition of French. And as we have already seen in chapter three, Article 133 of the BNA Act of 1867 guaranteed the equality of French and English in respect of the activities of the federal parliament and federal tribunals; the same principle applied to Quebec and, from 1870 on, to the province of Manitoba. This article 133, together with article 93 on education, contributed to the creation of a perception in Quebec of a "pact" between the nations or the two main linguistic communities, at least in numerical terms, in 1867.

This perception, whether justified or not, was dramatically undermined by events between 1885 and 1913: the second Métis rebellion, the hanging of Louis Riel, the abolition of French and religious schools in Manitoba in 1890, the absence of explicit recognition of the equality of French and English in the creation of Alberta and Saskatchewan, and rule 17 in Ontario in 1913. All these events seriously compromised a perception among many French Canadians that English and French Canadians could live side by side without threat to their institutions and languages. Trudeau himself pointed out that British-Canadian chauvinism had created French-Canadian nationalism. At the very least, a certain asymmetry in the recognition of the equality of French and English prompted a change of perception about the "pact" among many Quebec French Canadians. Consequently, the Official Languages Act of 1969, voted in as a result of the recommendations of the Commission on Bilingualism and Biculturalism, attempted to correct the asymmetry evident in the application of Article 133. More than twenty years later, according to the report of the Treasury Council for 1995–96, twenty-nine percent of positions in the federal public sector are occupied by Francophones.[2] In addition, the number of bilingual posts has risen to thirty-one percent, a peak.[3] The Official Languages Act, one of the feathers in the Trudeauist political cap, had an obvious impact, especially outside Quebec; to refuse to acknowledge this would be proof of bad faith. But in correcting a near-century of non-application of article 133, the Trudeau government had to apply *de facto* an affirmative-action policy to redress an institutionalized situation that marginalised French Canadians. In other words, by means of this policy, it was hoped to create a collective institutional space conducive to the flourishing of Francophones. Hence the idea that the notion of collective rights weighted equally with individual rights was already present in the Official Languages Law of 1969, in the sense that it was clearly a form of affirmative action for French Canadians. Thus, one of the first fundamental interventions by Pierre Elliott Trudeau in his role as prime minister implied in reality—and despite a certain rhetoric—not an opposition between individual and collective rights, but a certain balance between these two concepts.

MULTICULTURALISM

Since the 1960s, multiculturalism has become one of Canada's essential political factors. It echoed the problematic of biculturalism of the 1960s and the debates about the relations between French and English Canadians. The presence of a French and Catholic population raised the question of difference in a society in which a majority was English and Protestant. Nearly a century after Confederation, the tensions between French and English Canadians filled Canadians of varied origin, neither French nor Anglo-American, but ever more numerous, with the fear that an essential component of Canadian society could be overlooked, even marginalised. The most active group were the Ukrainians, who demanded recognition of a "third force."[4] Thus volume IV of the Laurendeau-Dunton (Bilingualism and Biculturalism) Commission dealt with the cultural contribution of "Other Canadians." Sixteen recommendations that sprang from the information contained in this volume were presented by the commissioners. And on 8 October 1971, Pierre Elliott Trudeau announced the federal government's intention to launch an initiative for the promotion of multiculturalism within a bilingual framework. Trudeau stated:

Multiculturalism in a bilingual framework seems to the Government to be the best way of preserving the cultural liberty of Canadians. A policy of this kind should serve to reduce the discrimination and jealousy engendered by cultural differences. In order for national unity to have a meaningful personal significance, it must be based upon the sense that each individual has of his own identity; this is how respect for others will be created and the desire to share ideas and ways of looking at things. A dynamic multicultural policy will help us create that self-confidence which could be the basis of a society where there will be the same justice for all....

In applying its policy of multiculturalism in a bilingual framework, the Government will offer aid in four different ways:

First, depending on the availability of resources, the Government will try to help all Canadian cultural groups who have shown the desire and will to develop their ability to expand and to contribute to Canadian life and who are in obvious need of assistance, whether this involves small, modest groups or large, well-organized ones.

Second, the Government will help members of any cultural group to overcome the cultural barriers that prevent them from participating fully in Canadian society.

Third, the Government will encourage meetings and exchanges between all cultural groups of Canada in the interests of national unity.

Fourth, the Government will continue to help immigrants to learn at least one of the official languages and to become integrated into Canadian society.[5]

Once again, it seems that this policy statement refers to collective categories. Insofar as multiculturalism was meant to fit into a bilingual framework, the principle was clearly to encourage the harmonious integration of groups of diverse origins into one or other (or both) national communities of European origin, since Aboriginal peoples were not considered as a founding nation in 1971. Promoting multiculturalism in the framework of bilingualism necessarily meant recognizing, to a certain degree, differences of context for people coming from different cultures and groups. There again seems to be in reality no conflict between the notion of collectivity and that of individual rights in Trudeau's policies.

THE WHITE PAPER ON ABORIGINAL PEOPLES

With the goal of achieving the objectives of a just society, and the sense of equality of its citizens, in 1969 the Government of Pierre Elliott Trudeau presented a White Paper on the question of native peoples. The White Paper proposed the gradual abolition of the Ministry of Indian Affairs and of the Indian Act over a period of five years. Provision was also made for the elimination of the status of "Indian." This programme took little heed of the claims of the Aboriginal peoples—especially the recognition of the treaties and the legitimacy of some territorial claims.

Since the late nineteenth century, the Aboriginal peoples had formed different associations.[6] The Nisga'a of British Columbia had been extremely militant as early as 1887. Later, two other associations were formed, the Allied Tribes of British Columbia in 1915 and the Fraternity of Native Peoples of British Columbia in 1931. In Ontario and Quebec, one of the first associations, formed in 1918, was the League of Indians of Canada. From the beginning of the Second World War on, associations proliferated: in 1939, the Indian Association of Alberta; in 1944, the Indians of Saskatchewan; in 1943, the Fraternity of North-American Indians.[7] To deal with the claims of the First Nations, two commissions of enquiry were formed, the first in 1946–48, the second in

1959–61. The work of these two commissions resulted in a new wave of militantism. So it was in the context of this militantism that the Trudeau Government presented its White Paper.

This document was received with considerable hostility. What made the government back off was the 1973 decision by the Supreme Court of Canada in the Calder case brought by the Nisga'a tribal council. Despite the vote against the Nisga'a Nation—four judges against, three in favor—the principle of native land rights, established by Royal Proclamation in 1763, was recognized. Subsequently, the following year, an office of native claims was formed, to undertake the massive task of dealing with native land claims. Nine years later, in 1982, Article 25 of the Charter of Rights and Freedoms and Section 35, which is not in the Charter, of the 1982 Constitutional Law recognized the "existing" rights of native peoples in Canada.[8] This time, it seemed that the combination of political circumstances had led Pierre Elliott Trudeau to recognize a collective claim—which he had to do in 1982 with the natives. The example of the native peoples made it clear once again that individuals cannot be divorced from their specific context. Thus, despite the emphasis on individual rights in Trudeau's discourse, three groups—the French Canadians, the non British, non-French and non-Aboriginal groups, and the First Nations— had to some extent a recognition of their collective reality in the institutions and laws of the Trudeau era.

NATIONALISM, CONSTITUTIONALISM, AND LIBERALISM

The high point of Trudeau's career was obviously the repatriation of the Canadian Constitution and the inclusion of a Charter of Rights and Freedoms. We have already seen that in the 1982 Constitutional Law, the collective rights of the aboriginal peoples are recognized in Sections 25 and 35. But this is not the only collectively oriented article. Article 15 on the right of equality, particularly sexual equality, is another example. Articles 16 to 22 on the official languages, and article 23 on the rights of instruction in the minority language constitute a form of protection for individuals belonging to specific collectivities targeted through the notion of "official" languages. Thus, despite Trudeau's strict rhetoric about individual rights, the 1982 Constitution and the Charter were rather a delicate balancing act between articles that fitted a strict perspective of individual rights (articles 1 to 15) and the articles with a clear collective angle.

Such an articulation is certainly not incompatible in principle with certain contemporary theories of justice. According to Guy Laforest (1993), the debate about theories of justice opposed in Canada those, like Janet Ajzenstat (1988), strictly concerned by individual rights to those, like Charles Taylor and James Tully, who have succeeded in showing the importance of placing the question of individual rights in specific, concrete contexts.[9] In the United States, a similar debate opposed liberals, like John Rawls and Ronald Dworkin, to communitarians, like Michael Walzer (Taylor, 1995). But is Rawls' *Theory of Justice* incompatible with a sense of the community?

In 1971, John Rawls argued that equality should be based on the principle that no group should have a long-term moral advantage over another:

> This account of the basis of equality calls for a few comments. First of all, it may be objected that equality cannot rest on natural attributes. There is no natural feature with respect to which all human beings are equal, that is, which everyone has (or which sufficiently many have) to the same degree. It might appear that if we wish to

hold a doctrine of equality, we must interpret it in another way, namely as a purely procedural principle. Thus to say that human beings are equal is to say that none has a claim to preferential treatment in the absence of compelling reasons. ...the essential equality is thought to be equality of consideration.[10]

This approach condemns all forms of discrimination, whether racial, sexual, religious, or linguistic, as well as economic, cultural, national, and social discrimination. Rawls' theory is based on a hypothetical social contract that assumes a temporary ignorance of our antecedents—the so-called "veil of ignorance." From this starting point, we must than reconstruct a social contract which presupposes sincere concern over the well-being of each participant, reasoning from the systematic elimination, given several possibilities, of the most reprehensible situation:

> Viewing the situation from the legislative stage, one may decide that the formation of paramilitary groups, which the passing of the statute may forestall, is a much greater danger to the freedom of the average citizen than being held strictly liable for the possession of weapons. Citizens may affirm the law as the lesser of two evils, resigning themselves to the fact that while they may be held guilty for things they have not done, the risks to their liberty on any other course would be worse. Since bitter dissensions exist, there is no way to prevent some injustices, as we ordinarily think of them, from occurring. All that can be done is to limit these injustices in the least unjust way.[11]

The principles involved here are 1) that each individual has the right to the greatest possible liberty if it is compatible with the liberty of others; 2) that social inequalities should be countered by the opening up of positions in conditions which favor equal opportunity; and 3) inequality is temporarily justified if it is a short-term means of avoiding worse situations. Thus, persecution, discrimination, and political oppression are incompatible with "equal" liberty. The rule of equal opportunity guarantees an equal chance of success, whatever the original social class or minority group. In Rawls' system, equality is seen in the context of a constant renewal of a contract aimed at limiting injustice. Therefore, the "veil of ignorance" used by Rawls as a starting point in his system does not exclude the eventuality of taking into consideration the concrete situation of individuals in order to favor an "equality of consideration":

> A doctrine of political economy must include an interpretation of the public good which is based on a conception of justice. It is to guide the reflections of the citizen when he considers questions of economic and social policy. He is to take up the perspective of the constitutional conventions or the legislative stage and ascertain how the principles of justice apply. A political opinion concerns what advances the good of the body politic as a whole and **invokes some criterion for the just division of social advantages.**[12]

In contrast to Trudeau, someone who really went *Against the Current* (1979) is Isaiah Berlin. Berlin, recalling Herder (Taylor, 1995), conceived a form of liberalism that could reflect the concrete struggles of individuals in their concrete social, national, cultural, or gendered reality (Taylor, 1995; Gray, 1995). Berlin criticized the chimerical "Whig" conception of history based on progress made exclusively by enlightened Anglo-American élites. On the contrary, a non-Whig definition of liberalism should constitute a manner of enhancing pluralism, including national pluralism. Federalism could be a means of accommodating different nations within the same state, none of those nations being considered "neutral." In that perspective, Guy Laforest (1993) is right to portray the Trudeau vision of federalism as extremely limited because of its denial of a plurality of nations in Canada. However, the idea defended by Laforest, that the communatarian approach of Taylor (1992) and other authors is preferable to the distributive justice approach of Rawls regarding the situation of national minorities, is debatable. Rawls' system, we think, should not be confused with authors like Janet Ajzenstat (1988), who clearly defines nationalism in a way that both the English language and Anglo-American culture are situated outside any nationalist sphere and are considered in an ontological fashion as neutral and transcendental to any "collectivist" reality. This is exactly where Anglo-American nationalisms are extremely efficient: in the negation of their own collective reality and the systemic projection on other cultures of the stereotype of "ethnic nationalism," which Anglo-America, including a very important form of Anglo-Canadian nationalism, refuses to acknowledge as a reality of its own culture.

This negation of its own nationalist reality is probably the most pernicious aspect of what we call ethnic liberalism, which was fully expressed in the Canadian context in 1990 and 1992 by the rejection of the Meech Lake and Charlottetown accords. We define "ethnic liberalism" as a form of liberalism, not to be confused with Rawls' system or Berlin's vision of history, that is based on the assumption of a moral superiority of Anglo-American culture, which is described as a "non-collectivist" culture. Despite the fact, as we have briefly described, that there are elements of collective rights in its own institutions, Pierre Elliott Trudeau rejected both Meech and Charlottetown on the basis that they were jeopardizing individual rights in Canada. Consequently, the former Prime Minister reproduced in politics a form of ethnic liberalism that became a key element of one very narrow version of Anglo-Canadian nationalism: the idea that Quebec and the First Nations are "collectivist," while the rest of Canada is supposedly "individualist." Thus, there is a clear pattern in the way Trudeau portrayed French-Canadian society in the 1950s and the way he rejected both the Meech Lake and Charlottetown accords.

MEECH LAKE AND CHARLOTTETOWN

We are not going to go into the details of a constitutional saga that galvanized an entire society for several years. We should note, however, that very few societies, if any, have succeeded in getting their citizens to discuss democratically the reworking of the social contract and the fundamental policy of the country without resorting to civil war. Trudeau was vehemently opposed to the Meech Lake and Charlottetown accords, and denounced with particular fervour the notion of "collective rights" applied in particular to French-speaking Quebeckers (Trudeau, 1992), Aboriginal peoples, and women.[13] In fact, the text of Meech Lake specified that

1. The Constitution of Canada shall be interpreted in a manner consistent with
    a. the recognition that the existence of French-speaking Canadians, centered in Quebec but also present elsewhere in Canada, and English-speaking Canadians, concentrated outside Quebec but also present in Quebec, constitutes a fundamental characteristic of Canada; and

b. the recognition that Quebec constitutes within Canada a distinct society.

2. The role of the Parliament of Canada and the provincial legislatures to preserve the fundamental characteristics of Canada referred to in paragraph (1)(a) is affirmed.

3. The role of the legislature and Government of Quebec to preserve and promote the distinct identity of Quebec referred to in paragraph (1)(b) is affirmed.[14]

The Charlottetown text is slightly different:

c. Quebec constitutes within Canada a distinct society, which includes a French speaking majority, a unique culture and a civil law tradition....[15]

Trudeau raised several legitimate questions about the concept of a "distinct society," although the reference to the First Nations in this passage seems odd considering Trudeau's own policy:

Does it refer to a French-Canadian collectivity that lives scattered throughout the whole of Canada? Obviously not, since the dominant ideology of Quebec could not care less about bilingualism in Canada and gave wholehearted support to the governments of Alberta and Saskatchewan when they suppressed Francophone rights that had been acquired even before these provinces entered Confederation in 1905.

Does it refer rather to the entire Quebec collectivity? Not that either, since that collectivity is called a "province" and its powers are already explicitly recognized by the Constitutional Act of 1867. It can only refer to a distinct collectivity within Quebec, but which one? Certainly not the English-speaking collectivity, since Quebec law denies that there can be collective rights in particular areas: schools and signs, for example. We must eliminate the aboriginal peoples, too, since they have been given to understand quite clearly that they cannot constitute a "distinct society" with the right to self-determination, since that word has already been reserved for Quebeckers of a different race.[16]

Yet by leaving the impression of an opposition between collective rights and individual rights in the context of the debates over the Meech Lake Accord and the Charlottetown Agreement, Trudeau once again contributed to the perception that French Canadians from Quebec are "collectivists." But we have seen that the institutions of the Trudeau era are themselves characterized by both collective aspects and individual rights. The question then is not to oppose these two notions but to find a solution that permits an acceptable balance. Was this balance fully achieved in 1982? With difficulty.

The entire theory of Pierre Elliott Trudeau is based on the assumption that French Canada was culturally nationalist and that Quebec nationalism since the Quiet Revolution systematically reproduced the marks of collective thinking. But it could be argued that a source of imbalance in the Constitution of 1982 sprang from the fact that protection for linguistic rights in articles 16–22 creates a space for development propitious to French Canada which was nonetheless earlier blamed by Trudeau for being collectively nationalist. If the logic of the argument depends on the principle of opposition between collective and individual rights, then why give to French Canada, and, incidentally, also to the English-Canadian collectivity (after all, the English language is also protected), what is being refused to French-speaking Quebeckers? Need we remind ourselves that Quebec nationalism—as Trudeau himself could not help pointing out, no doubt by accident—was created not necessarily because of a cultural essence but as a reaction to a particular British-Canadian nationalism. It was this interaction between different national visions that led finally to a political project articulated solely with respect to Quebec.

Therefore, would not a policy based strictly on the principle of individual rights have implied only the stating of these rights in articles 1–14 of the Charter without reference to linguistic rights? But insofar as these very linguistic rights—and, for example, a specific reference to the bilingual character of New Brunswick—along with the rights of the First Nations and the right to equality, were defined and inscribed in the Charter, the argument that the special situation of French-speaking Quebeckers could not be recognized without violating the principle of individual rights is unacceptable. The Charter already opened some collective perspectives, without which the principle of individual rights remains an abstraction. Meech and Charlottetown were, therefore, perfectly justifiable. However, in order to avoid the ambiguities of the notion of a distinct society while keeping the logic of a Charter based on two national languages, perhaps it would have been better to recognize openly the existence of a French-Canadian nation, coast to coast, but with a majority living in one "distinct" province. In the sometimes obsessive process of constructing a "single" Canadian nation since 1867, the least one can say is that pluralism, although partly inscribed in the Constitution of 1867 through the recognition of Francophone collectivity, was hardly applied. As a long-term consequence of the 1760 Conquest, an unequal union was formed in 1867 between two colonizers. Bringing the situation up to date with respect to French Canada and simultaneously to other groups would certainly not have been a systematic violation of individual rights, and would no doubt have been a creative means of defusing the nationalist crises we are now experiencing due to the obsession of national unity.

TRUDEAU, QUEBEC NATIONALISM, AND CANADIAN NATIONALISM

So the champion of the fight against "monolithism" found himself in the same camp as Lucien Bouchard and even Preston Manning in 1992. Far from being an accidental circumstance, this situation revealed a great similarity between Trudeau and, on the one hand, the Quebec nationalist, and, on the other, the English-Canadian nationalist.

As we have seen in chapter two, supporters of Trudeau share with the sovereigntists a metaphysical vision of Quebec in which Quebec collectively constituted a unidimensional society before the Quiet Revolution. The debate between Trudeau and Lucien Bouchard in February 1996 was very revealing. Both men accept the paradigm of the folk society before the Quiet Revolution and describe Quebec as a non-modern society until 1960. Like Bouchard (see the Declaration of Sovereignty in the *Globe and Mail*, 7 September 1995), Trudeau has a teleological concept of the history of Quebec, including a moment of salvation and purification that allowed the society to start from scratch, throwing out wholesale its past—a past symbolized in particular by Duplessis. But as Bourque, Duchastel, and Beauchemin (1994) have pointed out, Duplessism constituted a form of political discourse in which tradition and modernity were so tangled up that it was impossible to create an opposition between them.

This idea, according to which a complex intertwining of features are categorized as ideal-types of tradition and modernity, could be applied to the western world in general, if not to any society. We have already suggested that an extensive literature on the United States (Pocock, 1975), Great Britain, France, and Germany (Mayer, 1983) demonstrates the absence of linear development marked by a turning point specific to each country, as each supposedly passed from tradition to modernity, some before the others. Marcel Gauchet was right to emphasize the importance of the constant renewal of the old world into the new (Gauchet, 1985).

In this perspective, the way the Duplessis régime was described in Trudeau's articles was a gross caricature. Far from being an anachronism, Duplessis was simply a very ordinary conservative politician, overtaken on the right by contemporary American politicians like Joseph McCarthy. What's more, Duplessis would clearly be overtaken on the right today by American politicians like Pat Buchanan and Jesse Helms, and we would find in premiers Ralph Klein and Mike Harris his true spiritual sons.

Similarly unacceptable is this equally teleological vision of history propagated by the intellectual underlings of Trudeauism, such as Behiels (1985), or of some other stamp, such as Dion (1993), which charts a successive development of different liberal states since the nineteenth century. Thus the classic liberal state followed the developmental state; then came the welfare state. But the fact that in all the western democracies for at least the last twenty years the welfare state has been dismantled to make way for new forms of a classic liberal state shows once more the absurdity of this linear historicist view. Since the eighteenth century, different liberal projects have been constantly at odds with each other and have systematically realigned the orientation of the state. History is not a succession of stages but a multidimensional reality transformed by the actions of individuals and/or groups facing varied contexts and challenges (Hirschman, 1980, 1991, 1995).

Certainly this latter proposition could be debated in the light of postmodern and postcolonial literature. But in this book, the main purpose was to verify to what extent Trudeau, self-proclaimed adversary of monolithism, seems in fact to have ignored approaches resistant to holism and to collective explanations. And for forty years, the entire project of an apparently liberal society has been formulated in this contradiction. Thus Trudeau as one of the most influential "intellectuals" of the 1950s, as far as the creation of the myth of "monolithism" is concerned, was in some ways responsible for the appearance of a new identity in Quebec, based on the rejection of its complex past.

There is yet more. The republication of Trudeau's texts in *Against the Current*, most dating back to the 1950s, is an interesting phenomenon. A publisher decided to recycle the texts, dressed up as an analysis of end-of-the-century problems. In all areas of social science and law, an extremely rich and complex literature has been produced since 1960, both in English Canada and French Canada. Trudeau seems not to have read any of this, so he has never tried to step back and reconsider his own interpretations. Thus, the food for thought offered to hundreds of thousands of Canadians is old-fashioned, out of date, and, as we have shown in previous chapters, marked by a reductive, even simplistic, approach. Consequently, if there has ever been in Canadian political history—French as well as English—an enterprise from the dark ages, it is certainly this industry of recycling Trudeau. No Catholic priest, no politician, not even Duplessis has succeeded like Pierre Elliott Trudeau in contextualizing a people from a collection of concepts that are so badly reductionist and now constitute the core of a pernicious form of ethnic nationalism which could be referred to as ethnic liberalism, a form of nationalism that Preston Manning tries desperately to lead into the next century.

conclusion

"WE BRITISH CANADIANS POSSESS a sense of racial superiority which seems to be innate in us, and which we do not acknowledge even to ourselves." — *W. Eric Harris, in 1927, quoted in Ray Conlogue,* Impossible Nation.

Ethnic liberalism? Since the seventeenth and eighteenth centuries, a certain discourse, among many, has developed in Great Britain, the United States, and English Canada about the cultural superiority of the English-speaking world. This superiority is based on the assumption that individuality is recognized and protected only in the English-speaking world. But if freedom and individuality are universal realities, why should there be only one cultural expression of these realities? Could it be possible that the fight for freedom is multidimensional, all societies being characterized by the tension between individuals and groups? Thus, as Claude Denis has observed, the Lockean discourse on individual rights could simply be one form of expression of that fundamental opposition in all societies (Denis, 1997).

Several writers, under the umbrella of postmodernity, have challenged the pretension of Anglo-American or even French liberalism of being universal, although they themselves have a tendency to reduce liberalism to a single discourse while in fact (despite the predominance of the "Whig" discourse even outside the Anglo-American world), liberalism in its complexity is a constant clash of visions—as we have seen with the distinction between Rawls' and Berlin's visions of liberalism and what we call ethnic liberalism. In the same perspective, history should be viewed as a multidimensional reality, interpreted in light of the study of the context in which individuals have to act. The Canadian situation, and particularly the French-Canadian case, provides numerous examples of this multidimensionality, despite a tendency in the social science and history literature on French Canada to reduce the complexity of this society. For this reason, French Canadian society is a fascinating case to explore from the perspective of a dominant strand of multidisciplinary literature, namely post-colonialism.

As we mentioned in chapter two, according to Edward Said (1978), who used Foucault's notion of discourse as power, the Western discourse on the Orient was a simplistic and reductionist representation of complex cultures and societies by the systemic colonialist power/knowledge of Europe. There is little doubt that Said's thesis opened the door to a very creative literature on the Orient and numerous interpretations dealing with the multiple dimensions of complex societies. But if society is constantly changing and mainly characterized by the clash of its numerous dimensions, is it possible that orientalist discourse was developed not only in order to dominate the Orient but also to mask key dimensions of conflict in the western world?

In North America, it could be argued that the First Nations were the object of a discourse similar to Orientalism. But to some extent—and despite the fact that it was a society derived from a colonial empire—French Canadian society, for more than a century starting with Lord Durham, may also be viewed as the object of some Orientalism, with theories like that of "folk society." As we have seen in chapters one and two, this theory portrayed French Canada as a predominantly rural society for most of the twentieth century, while in fact French Canada has been massively urbanized and industrialized at least since the First World War (not to mention the fact that one million French Canadians moved to New England between 1850 and 1930 in search of jobs in factories). This phenomenon reveals that a reductionist discourse could also be applied to a society formed by settler-colonization. By simplistically representing colonized societies, or dominated cultures emanating from a colonialist power (like French Canada), a colonial discourse developed that associated ideas like tradition and collectivity with cultural inferiority. But tradition and a sense of belonging to a collectivity did not disappear anywhere—particularly not in so-called advanced societies—and found numerous forms of expression. This is a key element of the multidimensionality of both history and societies in the twentieth century.

In the case of the French-Canadian society, it is interesting to note that many French Canadians in Quebec, since the Quiet Revolution, had a tendency to tailor their identity from the reductionist representation of its past described in this book and elsewhere (Couture, 1991, 1996), thus forging this very interesting paradox: the more many Quebeckers believe some observers about their monolithic past, the more it seems that they want to form an independent state in order to complete their liberation from that past. Paradoxically, that could be Trudeau's main contribution and inheritance, combined with the fact that thirty years of Trudeauism clearly reinforced a very narrow vision of Anglo-Canadian nationalism.

At a different level, although the writers discussed in this book did not systematically consider gender, it is fascinating to observe how many feminist social scientists and feminists historians have deconstructed the myth of the "folk society" (Hamilton, 1996). Nevertheless, the usual stereotypes about French Canada are still widespread and the power of these exaggerated characterizations is astonishing.

In *Impossible Nation*, Ray Conlogue (1996) writes, "We will better appreciate Québec when we come to appreciate ourselves." Precisely: it seems that our main task in order to recreate a dialogue (McRoberts, 1997) is not the usual reductionist discourse on Quebec—as in James Macpherson's recent comparison between the American Civil War and the current situation in Quebec (Macpherson, 1998)—but the deconstruction and interpretation of a dominant form of nationalism in English Canada, which is mainly characterized by the denial of its own existence or by a grotesque representation of the French-Canadian society, a phenomenon brilliantly analyzed, for example, by Daniel Francis (1997).

Finally, one would probably argue against the thesis of ethnic liberalism, that Canada, contrary to Quebec, is "civic" because of multiculturalism. But such a statement is once again based on the premise that the English language and culture are neutral and disconnected from any colonial background (as if the only European colonialism that matters in Canadian history is French). The censuses of both 1991 and 1996 have revealed that, despite the fact Canadians of British origin are now a minority, an overwhelming majority of Canadians outside Quebec (eighty-seven percent) speak

English at home. It seems that multiculturalism, despite its good intentions, has mainly provided a frame for the democratization of assimilation. In a self-proclaimed multicultural society, what could possibly justify the legislative protection of any colonial language? The argument here is not to deny the international ascendancy of English as the most important second language of a majority of human beings on the globe. But in the context of a multicultural Canada, if one cannot justify any protection for the French language, what then could justify the protection of the English language over, in some parts of Canada, Chinese, German, or Ukrainian? Does multiculturalism make any sense without a policy of multilingualism (Edwards, 1995)?

To sum up, if one reads the collected and republished texts of Trudeau (Trudeau, 1996), one forms the distinct impression that Pierre Elliott Trudeau was indeed constantly on the point of succumbing to the culturalist temptation, thus to a generalizing and collective form of explanation. In this sense, Trudeau made a great contribution to the creation of a form of representation of Quebec, which is, paradoxically, at the centre of today's Quebec-nationalist project, based to some extent on a global refusal of a past perceived as monolithic. This past was not, however, monolithic. Elsewhere, by using, in contradiction with his own institutions, a definition of universal rights without reference to the specific situations of French Canadians and First Nations, Trudeau reinforced a particular kind of English-Canadian nationalism that finds its articulation in the appropriation of a liberal idea made out to be exclusively Anglo-American. The heritage Trudeau left is consequently heavily ambiguous and by now deeply embedded in the institutions of the country. In fact, these institutions systematically generate instability. Given the uncertain future of Canada and Quebec, the time is ripe for a serious debate on the ideological and institutional legacy of Trudeau, one that considers how this legacy may account for the *current* impasse.

notes

INTRODUCTION

1 Pierre Elliott Trudeau, "Politique fonctionnelle," *Cité libre* 1:1 (1950): 21.
2 "Politique fonctionnelle," 24.
3 Pierre Elliott Trudeau, *Against the Current: Selected Writings 1939–1996* (Toronto: McClelland and Stewart, 1996).

CHAPTER 1: THE ASBESTOS STRIKE

1 This group consisted of Gilles Beausoleil, Réginald Boisvert, Gérard Dion, Fernand Dumont, Jean Gérin-Lajoie, Charles A. Lussier, Gérard Pelletier, and Maurice Sauvé.
2 Pierre Elliott Trudeau, *The Asbestos Strike* (Montréal: Jour, 1956), 4.
3 *Asbestos Strike*, 5.
4 *Asbestos Strike*, 6.
5 *Asbestos Strike*, 7.
6 *Asbestos Strike*, 7.
7 *Asbestos Strike*, 8.
8 *Asbestos Strike*, 9.
9 *Asbestos Strike*, 9.
10 *Asbestos Strike*, 11; emphasis mine.
11 *Asbestos Strike*, 11.
12 *Asbestos Strike*, 11-12.
13 *Asbestos Strike*, 12.

14 *Asbestos Strike*, 12.

15 *Asbestos Strike*, 12.

16 *Asbestos Strike*, 38.

17 *Asbestos Strike*, 88.

18 *Asbestos Strike*, 90.

19 *Asbestos Strike*, 89.

20 *Asbestos Strike*, 89.

21 *Asbestos Strike*, 89.

22 *Asbestos Strike*, 84. Which means that Caucasians were thirty-seven percent unionized in a province well known for its racism against Chinese workers.

23 *Asbestos Strike*, 84.

24 *Asbestos Strike*, 31.

25 *Asbestos Strike*, 75.

26 *Asbestos Strike*, 74.

27 Richard Handler, *Nationalism and the Politics of Culture in Quebec* (Madison: University of Wisconsin Press, 1988). In particular, he writes, "The fact that different scholars and ideologues have imagined different folk societies for Quebec suggests that the model partakes more of the romantic and mythical than the objective and factual" (67).

28 This section on French-Canadian banks takes up an argument I have already discussed in my book *Le mythe de la modernisation du Québec* (Montréal: Meridian, 1991), 21-24.

29 Yves Bélanger and Pierre Fournier, *L'Entreprise québécoise* (Montréal: Hurtubise HMH, 1987).

30 *L'Entreprise québécoise*, 42.

31 *L'Entreprise québécoise*, 48.

32 Pierre Ansart, *Les Sociologies contemporaines* (Paris: Seuil, 1990), 9. See also Raymond Boudon (1979, 1984) and François Bourricaud (1982).

33 Bronislaw Malinowski, "Culture," in *Encylopaedia of the Social Sciences* Vol. 4, (New York, 1931), 625.

34 Pierre Elliott Trudeau, "Federalism, nationalism and reason," in *Federalism and French-Canadian Society* (Montréal: HMH, 1967), 214.

35 *Les Sociologies contemporaines*, 51.

36 Quoted in Raymond Boudon and François Bourricaud, *Dictionnaire critique de la sociologie*, (Paris: Presses universitaires de France, 1982), v.

37 *Les Sociologies contemporaines*, 79.

38 *Les Sociologies contemporaines*, 83.

39 *Les Sociologies contemporaines*, 89.

CHAPTER 2: THE NEW BETRAYAL OF THE INTELLECTUALS

1 Pierre Elliott Trudeau, "The new betrayal of the intellectuals," in *Federalism and French Canadian Society* (Montréal: HMH, 1967), 162.

2 "The new betrayal," 166.

3 "The new betrayal," 171.

4 "The new betrayal," 173.

5 "The new betrayal," 173.

6 "The new betrayal," 180; emphasis mine.

7 In Julien Benda, *The Betrayal of the Intellectuals* (Boston: Beacon Hill, 1955 [1928]).

8 "The new betrayal," 221.

9 This section is a reworking of a paper presented at the Sorbonne in Paris on 23 May 1996, at a meeting of the French Association for Canadian Studies.

10 Jocelyn Létourneau, "L'imaginaire historique des jeunes Québécois," *Revue d'histoire de l'Amérique française* 41:4 (1988), 555.

11 "L'imaginaire historique," 557 and 563.

12 Ronald Rudin, "Revisionism and the search for a normal society: a critique of the recent Quebec historical writing," *Canadian Historical Review* 73 (1992), 60.

13 Michel Foucault, "Qu'est-ce que les Lumières?" *Magazine littéraire* 309 (1993), 72.

CHAPTER 3: ÉTIENNE PARENT

1 The quotations from Étienne Parent in this chapter are taken from his eight speeches made between 1846 and 1852 to the members of the Canadian Institute, in Montreal and Quebec City. The first five

lectures were first published in several newspapers in 1846, 1847, and 1848, and republished in 1850 in a book entitled *Discours*. The last three lectures were first published in newspapers in 1852 and finally reproduced in *La littérature canadienne de 1850 à 1860*. See the bibliography for the list of different editions. All the quotations in this chapter are taken from *Discours* and *La littérature canadienne* and have been translated.

2 Gérard Bergeron, *Lire Étienne Parent: Notre premier intellectuel (1802-1874)* (Quebec: University of Quebec Press, 1994).

3 For a review of the literature, see Fernande Roy, *Progrès, Harmonie, Liberté: Le libéralisme des milieux d'affaires francophones au tournant du siècle* (Montréal: Boréal, 1988).

4 Louis Nourry, *La pensée économique d'Étienne Parent: 1822-1852* (Master's thesis in History, University of Montreal, 1969), 1.

5 *Lire Étienne Parent*, 3 (note 1).

6 Fernand Ouellet, "Étienne Parent et le mouvement du catholicisme social," *Bulletin des recherches historiques* 61, 3: 99.

7 Benoît Bernier, "A propos d'Étienne Parent," *Revue d'histoire de l'Amérique française* 27, 1 (June 1973): 87.

8 Jean-Charles Falardeau, *Étienne Parent: 1802-1874* (Montréal: La Presse, 1975), 13.

9 Robert Major, *Jean Rivard ou l'art de réussir* (Québec: Presses Universitares de Laval, 1991), 23-67.

10 *Jean Rivard*, 23-67.

11 "A propos d'Étienne Parent," 87.

12 Jean-Pierre Wallot, *Un Québec qui bougeait: Patronage et pouvoir* (Montréal: Boréal Express, 1973).

13 *Un Québec qui bougeait*.

14 "À propos d'Étienne Parent," 87.

15 *Lire Étienne Parent*, 11.

16 *Lire Étienne Parent*, 12.

17 *Le Canadien*, 15 January 1823, quoted in *Étienne Parent: 1802-1874*, 12.

18 *Le Canadien*, 19 February 1823; *Le Canadien*, 18 February 1824; quoted in *Étienne Parent: 1802-1874*, 53, 60.

19 Benoît Bernier, *Les idées politiques d'Étienne Parent* (Thèse de D.E.S. en histoire, Université Laval, 1971), 71, 72, 73, 75.

20 *Les idées politiques d'Étienne Parent*, 50.

21 *Lire Étienne Parent*, 23.

22 *Les idées politiques d'Étienne Parent*, 41

23 "À propos d'Étienne Parent," 89.

24 Le Canadien, October 28th 1835, quoted in *Étienne Parent: 1802-1874*, 41.

25 Louis Nourry, *La pensée politique d'Étienne Parent: 1831-1852* (Doctoral thesis, University of Montreal, 1971).

26 *Lire Étienne Parent*, 51.

27 *Le Canadien*, 13 February 1837.

28 *Lire Étienne Parent*, 63.

29 *Lire Étienne Parent*, 63.

30 Ramsay Cook, *Le Canada: étude moderne* (Toront:, Clarke, 1981).

31 *Le Canada: étude moderne*, 53.

32 *Lire Étienne Parent*, 107.

33 *Le Canada: étude moderne*, 56.

34 "À propos d'Étienne Parent," 89.

35 "À propos d'Étienne Parent," 89.

36 *Étienne Parent: 1802-1874*, 24 (in the Saguenay riding with a majority of 3 votes).

37 *Étienne Parent: 1802-1874*, 25.

38 *Les idées politiques d'Étienne Parent*, 2-3.

39 *Étienne Parent: 1802-1874*, 25.

40 *Étienne Parent: 1802-1874*, 25.

41 *Jean Rivard*, 38.

42 *Jean Rivard*, 39.

43 *Jean Rivard*, 41.

44 Patrick Verley, *La Révolution industrielle: 1760-1870* (Paris: M A Éditions, 1985).

45 *La Révolution industrielle*

46 *La Révolution industrielle*

47 Yvan Lamonde, *Gens de parole. Conférences publiques, essais, débats à l'Institut Canadien de Montréal, 1845-1871* (Montréal: Boréal, 1990).

48 *Le Canadien*, 4 February 1846; *La Minerve*, 23 November 1846; *Le Canadien*, 27 November 1846; *Mélanges religieux* IX, (1846): 87-90; *La Minerve*, 27 September 1847; *Le Canadien*, 6–7 October 1847; *La*

Minerve, March 1848; *La Minerve*, 18 December 1848; *L'Avenir*, 27–30 December 1848; *L'Avenir*, 3 January 1849; *Le Canadien*, 8, 10, 12 January 1849.

49 *Lire Étienne Parent*, 174.

50 *Lire Étienne Parent*, 175.

51 *Lire Étienne Parent*, 284.

52 *Lire Étienne Parent*, 161.

53 See Joyce Appleby, *Capitalism and a New Social Order* (New York and London: New York University Press, 1984) and J.G. Pocock, *The Machiavellian Moment: Florentine Political Thought and the Atlantic Republican Tradition* (Princeton: Princeton University Press, 1975).

54 Point number 6 is duplicated in the original; we have retained the numbering of Parent's first edition.

55 *Étienne Parent: 1802-1874*, 26.

56 *La Voix du Golfe*, July 14th 1868, quoted in Urbain Blanchet, *Étienne Parent, ses opinions pédagogiques et religieuses* (Doctoral thesis, Laval University, 1965), 204–208.

57 *Étienne Parent, ses opinions*, 204–208.

58 Hector Fabre, *L'Événement*, 14 December 1874.

59 Joseph Schull, *Laurier* (Montréal: HMH, 1968), 528.

60 Yvan Lamonde, *Louis-Antoine Dessaulles: Un seigneur libéral et anticlérical* (Montréal: Fides), 232–233.

61 Raoul Dandurand, *Les mémoires du sénateur Dandurand* (Québec: Presses de l'Université Laval, 1967).

62 James Huston, ed., *Répertoire national ou recueil de littérature national*, 2e édition, 4 volumes (Montréal, 1893).

63 *Répertoire national*, 365-366.

64 Benjamin Sulte, *Mélanges historiques*, 21 volumes (Montréal: Ducharme, 1918 to 1932).

65 *Étienne Parent* (volume 14 of Mélanges historiques, republished in 1928 by Édouard Garant).

66 Gérard Parizeau, "Mon ami Étienne Parent" in *L'Action universitaire* II, 3 (February 1936): 50-51. Mention should also be made of the appearance in the same year of a text by Parent's grandson, Léon Gérin, son of Antoine Gérin–Lajoie, 'Étienne Parent, 1801-

1974—Journaliste, député, fonctionnaire, économiste' in *La vie nicolétaine* IV, 7 (September 1936): 57-59.

67   Monseigneur Camille Roy, *Manuel d'histoire de la littérature canadienne de langue française* (Montréal: Beauchemin, 1939), 26–29.

68   Monseigneur Émile Chartier, *Au Canada français: la vie de l'esprit* (Montréal: Valiquette, 1941), 73.

69   Paul-Eugène Gosselin, *Étienne Parent (1802-1874)*, (Montréal and Paris: Fides, 1964).

70   François-Albert Angers, "Naissance de la pensée économique au Canada français" in *Revue d'histoire de l'Amérique française* XV, 2 (September, 1961): 204-229.

71   Arthur Saint-Pierre, "La littérature sociale canadienne-française avant la confédération" in *Mémoires de la société royale du Canada* June 1950: 67-94.

72   Mason Wade, *The French Canadians, Volume 2* (Toronto: MacMillan, 1969), 154-170.

73   *La pensée politique d'Étienne Parent.*

74   "À propos d'Étienne Parent," 87.

75   *Étienne Parent, ses opinions*, 204–208.

76   *Étienne Parent: 1802-1874.*

77   Gilles Gallichan, *Livret politique au Bas-Canada: 1791-1849* (Sillery: Septentrion, 1991), 171.

78   Claude Doyon, "Étienne Parent (1802-1874)" in *Figures de la philosophie québécoise après les troubles de 1837* (Montréal, 1985), 203.

79   *Lire Étienne Parent.* See also Stéphane Kelly, *La petite loterie* (Montréal: Boréal, 1997).

80   *The asbestos strike.*

81   *The asbestos strike*, 15.

82   André Vachet, *L'idéologie libérale* (Paris: Anthropos, 1971).

83   Louis Hartz, *The Liberal Tradition in America* (New York: Bruce and World, 1955).

84   C.B.Macpherson, *The Life and Times of Liberal Democracy* (Oxford: Oxford University Press, 1977).

85   Charles Taylor, *Multiculturalisme* (Paris: Auber, 1994).

CHAPTER 4: THE JUST SOCIETY

1   "The values of a just society" in *Towards a Just Society, The Trudeau Years* (Markham: Viking, 1990), 358–359.

2   "Federal public office has never been so Francophone and bilingual" in *Le Franco* 11 October 1996: 1.

3   "Federal public office has never been so Francophone."

4   Yasmeen Abu-Laban, "The Politics of Race and Ethnicity: Multiculturalism as a Contested Arena" in *Canadian Politics*, James P. Bickerton and Alain G. Gagnon, eds. (Peterborough: Broadview, 1994), 242-263.

5   "Current affairs. Canadian culture." *Debates in the House of Commons* 8 October 1971: 8546. My emphasis.

6   Olive Dickason, *Canada's First Nations: A History of Founding Peoples from Earliest Times* (Toronto: McClelland and Stewart, 1992).

7   *Canada's First Nations.*

8   Gerald R. Alfred, *Heeding the Voices of our Ancestors* (Toronto: Oxford University Press, 1995).

9   James Tully, *Strange Multiplicity, Constitutionalism in an Age of Diversity* (Cambridge: Cambridge University Press, 1995). Charles Taylor, *Réconcilier les solitudes* (Québec: Presses de l'Université Laval, 1992). See also Guy Laforest, *De la prudence* (Montréal: Boréal, 1993).

10 John Rawls, *A Theory of Justice* (Cambridge: The Belknap Press of Harvard University Press, 1971), 507.

11 *A Theory of Justice,* 242.

12 *A Theory of Justice,* 259.

13 André Picard. "Trudeau denounces Accord" in *The Globe and Mail* 2 October 1992.

14 "The Meech Lake Accord." Government Document (1987): 31.

15 "The Charlottetown agreement." Government Document (September 1992): A-3.

16 Pierre Elliott Trudeau, "De la pauvreté de la pensée nationaliste au Québec" in *L'Actualité* 17:15 (1 October 1992), I-VIII.

bibliography

PUBLICATIONS OF
PIERRE ELLIOTT TRUDEAU

Trudeau, Pierre Elliott. "Politique fonctionnelle." *Cité libre* 1: 1 (juin 1950): 20-24.

———. *Le fédéralisme et la société canadienne-française*. Montréal: HMH, 1967.

———. *Réponses de Pierre Elliott Trudeau*. Montréal: Éditions du Jour, 1968.

———. "Current affairs. Canadian culture." *Debates in the House of Commons* 8 October 1971: 8546.

———. *Trudeau: Conversation with Canadians*. Toronto: University of Toronto Press, 1972.

———. *Lac Meech: Trudeau parle*. Montréal: Hurtubise HMH, 1989.

———. "De la pauvreté de la pensée nationaliste au Québec." *L'Actualité* (supplement) 17:15 (1 October 1992): I-VIII.

———. "Trudeau says scare scenario 'a lie'." P. Van de Wille, translator. *The Globe and Mail* 2 Octobre 1992.

———. "Ce gâchis mérite de recevoir un gros NON." Excerpt from a lecture on 1 October 1992. *La Presse* 2 October 1992.

———. "Trudeau to Robertson: `So where is the demagogy?'" *The Globe and Mail* 21 October 1992.

———. *Mémoires politiques*. Montréal: Le Jour, 1993.

———. "J'accuse Lucien Bouchard." *La Presse* 3 February 1996: B3.

———. "Trudeau à Bouchard: `Je ne vous souhaite pas de réussir, mais je vous dis: Dieu vous garde!'" *La Presse* 17 February 1996: B3.

———. *Against the Current: Selected Writings 1939-1996.* Toronto: McClelland and Stewart, 1996.

———, ed. *La grève de l'amiante.* Montréal: Éditions du Jour, 1970 (1956).

Axworthy, Thomas S. and Pierre E. Trudeau. *Les années Trudeau.* Montréal: Le Jour, 1990.

Axworthy, Thomas S. and Pierre E. Trudeau. *Towards a Just Society.* Markham: Viking, 1990.

ARTICLES ABOUT PIERRE ELLIOTT TRUDEAU

The Globe and Mail

"Trudeau sings old tune." Hugh Windsor, 22 September 1992.

"Deck the halls with maple leaves and try not to look unpatriotic." Jeffrey Simpson, 22 September 1992.

"Old colleagues may drift away, but Mr. Trudeau holds his course." Jeffrey Simpson, 23 September 1992.

"Trudeau's really looking `for a way to show his remorse'." Pauline Couture, 29 September 1992.

"Mysticism and politics Trudeau speaks." Robert Sheppard, 1 October 1992.

"Trudeau denounces accord." André Picard, 2 October 1992.

"Trudeau stands alone and defiant." Jeffrey Simpson, 3 October 1992.

"The country may yet succeed in unifying itself with one big No." Lysiane Gagnon, 10 October 1992.

"Quinze ans n'ont pas suffi à réparer le tort que Trudeau a fait au Québec." 10 February 1996.

The Calgary Herald

"Trudeau unleashes his thunder on Quebec." Canadian Press, 22 September 1992.

"Accord threat to equality: Trudeau." Canadian Press, 2 October 1992.

"Pierre Trudeau right about distinct society." Tim Sandberg, 19 October 1992.

Le Devoir

"Trudeau soulève une tempête au Canada, une brise au Québec." Chantal Hébert, 22 September 1992.

La Presse

"Le Québec fait 'chanter' le Canada anglais depuis 22 ans, dit Trudeau."
Maurice Girard, 21 September 1992.

"L'entente de Charlottetown." La Presse, 4 septembre 1992.

Le Franco

"La fonction publique fédérale n'a jamais été aussi francophone et
bilingue." Le Franco, 11 octobre 1996.

PUBLICATIONS OF ÉTIENNE PARENT

"L'industrie considérée comme moyen de conserver notre nationalité."
First published in Le Canadien 4 février 1846. Republished in
Répertoire national 1848-1850 (James Huston, ed.), volume IV: 3-21.
Subsequently published by Étienne Parent as Discours (Montréal:
Lovell and Gibson, 1850), pp. 3-21.

"Importance de l'étude de l'économie politique." First published in La
Minerve 23 November 1846, then in Le Canadien, 27 novembre
1846. Republished in Répertoire national 1848-1850 (James Huston,
ed.), volume IV: 21-44. Subsequently published by Étienne Parent
as Discours (Montréal: Lovell and Gibson, 1850), pp. 21-44.

"Du travail chez l'homme." First published in La Minerve 27 September
1847, then in Le Canadien 6-7 October 1847. Republished in
Répertoire national 1848-1850 (James Huston, ed.), volume IV: 44-
79. Subsequently published by Étienne Parent as Discours
(Montréal: Lovell and Gibson, 1850), pp. 44-79.

"Considérations sur notre système d'éducation populaire, sur l'éducation
en général et sur les moyens législatifs d'y pourvoir." First published
in La Minerve 1 March 1848, then in Mélanges religieux XI (1848):
48-49. Republished in Répertoire national 1848-1850 (James Huston,
ed.), volume IV: 316-357. Subsequently published by Étienne Parent
as Discours (Montréal: Lovell and Gibson, 1850), pp. 117-157.

"Du prêtre et du spiritualisme dans leurs rapports avec la société." First
published in La Minerve 18 December 1848, then in L'Avenir 27, 30
December 1848 and 3 January 1849, and then in Le Canadien 8, 10,
12 January 1849. Republished in Répertoire national 1848-1850 (James
Huston, ed.), volume IV: 80-117. Subsequently published by Étienne
Parent as Discours (Montréal: Lovell and Gibson, 1850), pp. 80-117.

"De l'importance et des devoirs du commerce." First published in *Le
   Canadien* 19 January 1852, then in *La Minerve* 3 February 1852, and
   then in *Mélanges religieux* XV (1852): 34-36.
Republished as a brochure (E.R. Fréchette, Québec, 1852), 22 pp.
   Subsequently published in *La littérature canadienne de 1850 à 1860*
   (Foyer canadien, 1863), volume I: 7-35.
"De l'intelligence dans ses rapports avec la société." First published in
   two parts in *Le Canadien* 26, 28 January and 11, 13 February 1852,
   then in *La Minerve* 6, 10, 17, 20 février 1852. Republished as a
   brochure (E.R. Fréchette, Québec, 1852), 67 pp. Subsequently
   published in *La littérature canadienne de 1850 à 1860* (Foyer canadien, 1863), volume I: 72-178.
"Considérations sur le sort des classes ouvrières." Published as a
   brochure (E.R. Fréchette, Québec, 1852), 26 pp. Subsequently
   published in *La littérature canadienne de 1850 à 1860* (Foyer canadien, 1863), volume I: 37-75.

OTHER BOOKS AND ARTICLES

Abrams, Philip. *Historical Sociology*. New York: Cornell University
   Press, 1982.
Abu-Laban, Yasmeen. "The Politics of Race and Ethnicity:
   Multiculturalism as a Contested Arena." *Canadian Politics*. James
   P. Bickerton and Alain G. Gagnon, eds. Petersborough: Broadview,
   1994.
Ajzenstat, Janet. *The Political Thought of Lord Durham*. Kingston and
   Montreal: McGill-Queen's University Press, 1988.
———— and Peter J. Smith. *Canada's Origins: Liberal, Tory or
   Republican?* Ottawa: Carleton University Press, 1995.
Amselle, Jean-Loup. *Nations et Nationalismes*. Paris: La Découverte,
   1995.
Angus, Ian. *A Border Within: National Identity, Cultural Plurality and
   Wilderness*. Montreal and Kingston: McGill-Queen's University
   Press, 1997.
Ansart, Pierre. *Les sociologies contemporaines*. Paris: Seuil, 1990.
Appleby, Joyce. *Capitalism and a New Social Order: The Republican
   Vision of the 1790s*. New York and London: New York University
   Press, 1984.

Aron, Raymond. *Les étapes de la pensée sociologique*. Paris: Gallimard, 1967.

Bates, Robert and Margaret Levi, eds. "The Political Economy of French and English Development." *Politics and Society*, 16:2-3: 159-410.

Behiels, Michael A. *Prelude to Quebec's Quiet Revolution: Liberalism versus neo-nationalism*. Montréal and Kinsgton: McGill-Queen's University Press, 1985.

Bédarida, François. *L'Angleterre triomphante*. Paris: Hatier, 1974.

Bélanger, André. J. *L'apolitisme des idéologies québécoises*, Québec: Presses de l'Université Laval, 1974.

Bélanger, Yves and Pierre Fournier. *L'entreprise québécoise. Développement historique et dynamique contemporaine*, LaSalle: Hurtubise HMH, 1987.

Berger, Carl. *The Sense of Power: Studies in the Ideas of Canadian Imperialism 1867-1914*. Toronto: University of Toronto Press, 1970.

————. *The Writing of Canadian History*. Toronto: University of Toronto Press, 1977.

Bergeron, Gérard. *Du duplessisme à Trudeau et Bourassa, 1956-1971*. Montréal: Parti pris, 1971.

Bergeron, Gérard. *Lire Étienne Parent. Notre premier intellectuel (1802-1874)*. Québec: Presses de l'Université du Québec, 1994.

Berlin, Isaiah. *Against the Current*. London: Hogarth Press, 1979.

Bernier, Benoît. "À propos d'Étienne Parent" in *Revue d'histoire de l'Amérique française* 27:1 (juin 1973): 87.

————. *Les idées politiques d'Étienne Parent*. Thèse de D.E.S. en histoire, Université Laval, 1971.

Bétourné, Olivier and Aglaia I. Hartig. *Penser l'histoire de la Révolution*, Paris: La Découverte, 1989.

Black, Conrad. *Duplessis*. Toronto: McClelland and Stewart, 1977.

Blanchet, Urbain, *Étienne Parent. Ses opinions pédagogiques et religieuses*. Thèse de D.E.S., Université Laval, 1965.

Bothwell, Robert, Ian Drummond, and John English. *Canada Since 1945: Power, Politics, and Provincialism*. Toronto: University of Toronto Press, 1981.

Bonin, Hubert. "La Révolution française a-t-elle bloqué le développement économique." *L'histoire* 77: 98-100.

Boudon, Raymond. *La logique du social*. Paris: Hachette, 1979.

————. *La place du désordre*. Paris: Presses universitaires de France, 1984.

Boudon, Raymond and François Bourricaud. *Dictionnaire critique de la sociologie*. Paris: Presses universitaires de France, 1982.

Bourque, Gilles, Jules Duchastel and Jacques Beauchemin. *La société libérale duplessiste*. Montréal: Presses de l'Université de Montréal, 1994.

Bradbury, Bettina. "The Family Economy and Work in an Industrializing City : Montreal in the 1970's." *Communications historiques*. Ottawa: Société historique du Canada, 1979.

Breton, Albert, Raymond Breton, Claude Bruneau, Yvon Gauthier, Marc Lalonde, Maurice Pinard and Pierre E. Trudeau. "Manifeste pour une politique fonctionnelle." *Cité libre* 67 (mai 1964).

Bumsted, J.M.. *The Peoples of Canada*. Toronto: Oxford University Press, 1992.

Christian, William and Sheila Grant, eds. *The George Grant Reader*. Toronto: University of Toronto Press, 1998.

Clarkson, Stephen. *Canada and the Reagan Challenge: Crisis and Adjustment 1981-1985*. Toronto: Lorimer, 1985.

Clarkson, Stephen and Christine McCall. *Trudeau and Our Times, Volume 1: The Magnificent Obsession*. Toronto: McClelland and Stewart, 1990.

———. *Trudeau and Our Times, Volume 2: The Heroic Desillusion*, Toronto: McClelland and Stewart, 1994.

Conlogue, Ray. *Impossible Nation: The Longing for Homeland in Quebec and Canada*. Stratford: Mercury Press, 1996.

Cook, Ramsay. *Le Canada: étude moderne*. Toronto: Clarke, 1981.

Cornell, Paul G. et al. *Canada: Unité et diversité*. Toronto: Holt, Rinehart, Winston, 1971 (1968).

Courville, Serge and Normand Séguin. *Le monde rural québécois au XIXe siècle*, Ottawa: Société historique du Canada, 1989.

Couture, Claude and Jean-François Cardin. *Histoire du Canada: Espace et différences*. Québec: Presses de l'Université Laval, 1996.

———. *Le mythe de la modernisation du Québec*. Montréal: Méridien, 1991.

———. "The Conquest of 1760 and the Problem of the Transition to Capitalism." *Reappraisals in Canadian History*. Angus D. Gilbert, ed. Scarborough: Prentice-Hall, 1993.

Couture, Claude and Claude Denis. "La captation du couple tradition-modernité par la sociographie québécoise." *Canada: Theorical*

Discourse/Discours théorique. Terry Goldie, Carmen Lambert and
   Rowland Lorimer, eds. Montréal: Association d'études canadi-
   ennes, 1994.

Couture, Claude and Linda Cardinal. "Liberalism, Nationalism,
   Pluralism: Political Representation and Nation-Building in Canada
   before and after the Québec Referendum." *Constitutional
   Forum/Forum constitutionnel* 7:2-3 (1996): 73-79.

Crafts, F.R. "British Economic Growth: Review of the Evidence," *The
   Economic History Review*, 36:3 (May 1983): 177-199.

Crouzet, François. *De la supériorité de l'Angleterre sur la France.
   L'économique et l'imaginaire*. Paris: Perrin, 1985.

——. "Angleterre et France au 18e siècle: Essai d'analyse comparée
   de deux croissances." *Cahiers d'histoire* XII (1967): 67-85.

Dandurand, Raoul. *Les mémoires du sénateur Dandurand*. Québec:
   Presses de l'Université Laval, 1967.

Denis, Claude. *We are not you: First Nations and Canadian Modernity*.
   Peterborough: Broadview, 1997.

Dickason, Olive P. *Canada's First Nations*. Toronto: McClelland and
   Stewart, 1992.

Disselkamp, Annette. *L'éthique protestante de Max Weber*. Paris: Presses
   universitaires de France, 1994.

Dion, Léon. *Québec, 1945-2000, Tome II, les intellectuels et le temps de
   Duplessis*. Sainte-Foy: Presses de l'Université Laval, 1993.

Doyon, Claude. "Étienne Parent (1802-1874)." *Figures de la philosophie
   québécoise après les troubles de 1837*. Montréal: UQAM, 1985.

Drabble, Margaret, ed. *The Oxford Companion to English Literature*.
   Oxford: Oxford University Press, 1995.

Dumont, Fernand et al. *Les idéologies au Canada français (1850-1900)*.
   Québec: Presses de l'Université Laval, 1971.

——. *Les idéologies au Canada français (1900-1929)*. Québec: Presses
   de l'Université Laval, 1974.

——. *Les idéologies au Canada français (1929-1939)*. Québec: Presses
   de l'Université Laval, 1978.

——. *Les idéologies au Canada français (1940-1976)*. 3 volumes.
   Québec: Presses de l'Université Laval, 1979.

Dumont, Fernand. *Genèse de la société québécoise*, Montréal: Boréal,
   1993.

Durand, Jean-Pierre and Robert Weil. *Sociologie contemporaine*, Paris: Migot, 1989.

Dworkin, Ronald. *Taking Rights Seriously*. Cambridge: Harvard University Press, 1977.

Edwards, John. *Multilingualism*. London: Penguin Books, 1995.

Engelstad, Diane et al. *Nation to Nation. Aboriginal Sovereignity and the Future of Canada*. Concord: Anansi, 1992.

Fabre, Hector, *L'Événement* 14 décembre 1874.

Falardeau, Jean-Charles. "L'origine et l'ascension des hommes d'affaires dans la société canadienne-française." *Recherches sociographiques* 6:1 (1963): 33-45.

Falardeau, Jean-Charles. *Étienne Parent: 1802-1874*. Montréal: La Presse, 1975.

Fanon, Frantz. *Les damnés de la terre*. Paris: Maspero, 1961.

―――. "National culture." *The Post-Colonial Studies Reader*. Bill Ashcroft, Gareth Griffiths, Helen Tiffin, eds. London and New York: Routledge, 1995.

Finlay, J.L. and D.N. Sprague. *The Structure of Canadian History*. Scarborough: Prentice-Hall, 1989 (1979).

Forbes, H.D. "Hartz-Horowitz at Twenty: Nationalism and Socialism in Canada and the U.S." CJPS/RCSP, XX (juin 1987): 287-315.

Foucault, Michel. "Qu'est-ce que les Lumières." *Magazine littéraire* 309 (1993): 61-73.

Fournier, Marcel. *L'entrée dans la modernité*. Montréal: St-Martin, 1986.

Francis, Daniel. "How our schools taught us to look down on Quebeckers." *Globe and Mail* 13 September 1997, D3

Francis, R. Douglas, Richard Jones and Donald B. Smith. *Destinies*, Toronto: Holt, Rinehart and Winston, 1988.

Fukuyama, Francis. *La fin de l'histoire et le dernier homme*. Paris: Fayard, 1991.

Gagnon, Lysiane. "Void left by the collage of the Catholicism remains unfilled." *Globe and Mail* 4 May 1996, D3.

Gallichan, Gilles. *Livret politique au Bas-Canada: 1791-1849*. Sillery: Septentrion, 1991.

Garigue, Philippe. "Evolution et continuité dans la société rurale canadienne-française." *La société canadienne-française*. M. Rioux et Y. Martin, eds. Montréal: HMH, 1971.

Garraty, John A. *The Great Depression*, New York: Anchor Books, 1987.

Gash, Norman. *Aristocracy and People, Britain 1815-1865*. London: Edward Arnold, 1979.

Gauchet, Marcel. *Le désenchantement du monde*. Paris: Presses universitaires de France, 1985.

Geertz, Clifford, ed. *Old Societies and New States*, London: Free Press of Glencoe, 1963.

Gellner, Ernest. *Thought and Change*. London: Meidenfeld and Nicolson, 1964.

Gosselin, Paul-Eugène. *Étienne Parent (1802-1874)*. Montréal and Paris: Fides, 1964.

Grant, George. *Lament for a Nation*. Ottawa: Carleton University Press, 1978 (1970).

Gray, John. *Isaiah Berlin*. New York: Harper Collins, 1995.

Greenfeld, Liah. *Nationalism. Five Roads to Modernity*. Cambridge: Harvard University Press, 1992.

Guindon, Hubert. "The Social Evolution of Quebec Reconsidered." *French-Canadian Society*. Volume 1. Toronto and Montréal: McClelland and Stewart, 1964.

————. "L'évolution de la société canadienne-française." *La société canadienne-française*. Marcel Rioux et Yves Martin, eds. Montréal: HMH, 1971.

————. *Tradition, modernité et aspiration nationale de la société québécoise*. Montréal: Saint-Martin, 1990.

Guttsman, W.L. *The British Political Elite*. London: McGibbon, 1965.

Gwyn, Richard. *The Northern Magus: Pierre Trudeau and Canadians*. Toronto: McClelland and Stewart, 1980.

Hamilton, Roberta. *Gendering the Vertical Mosaic: Feminist Perspectives on Canadian Society*. Mississauga: Copp Clark Ltd., 1996.

Handler, Richard. *Nationalism of the Politics of Culture in Québec*. Madison: University of Wisconsin Press, 1988.

Hartz, Louis. *The Liberal Tradition in America*. New York: Bruce and World, 1955.

Hirschman, Albert O. *Les passions et les intérêts*. Paris: Presses universitaires de France, 1980.

————. *Deux siècles de rhétorique réactionnaire*. Paris: Fayard, 1991.

————. *A Propensity to Self-Subversion*. Cambridge: Harvard University Press, 1995.

Hobsbawn, Eric and Terence Ranger, eds. *The Invention of Tradition.*
Cambridge: Cambridge University Press, 1983.

Horowitz, Gad. *Canadian Labour in Politics.* Toronto: University of
Toronto Press, 1968.

Hugues, Everett C. *Rencontre de deux mondes.* Montréal: Lucien
Parizeau, 1945.

———— and Margaret L. McDonald. "French and English in the
Economic Structure of Montreal." *Canadian Journal of Economics
and Political Science* 7, 4 (novembre 1941): 493-505.

Huston, James, ed. *Répertoire national ou recueil de littérature nationale.*
2e édition, 4 volumes. Montréal: NP, 1893.

Kedourie, Elie. *Nationalism.* 4th edition. Oxford: Brail Blackwell, 1993.

Kelly, Stéphane. *La petite loterie.* Montréal: Boréal, 1997.

Kymlicka, Will. *Liberalism, Community and Culture.* Oxford: Oxford
University Press, 1989.

————. *Multicultural Citizenship.* Toronto: Oxford University Press,
1995.

Laforest, Guy. *Trudeau et la fin du rêve canadien.* Québec: Septentrion,
1992.

————. *De la prudence.* Montréal: Boréal, 1993.

Lamonde, Yvan. *Gens de parole. Conférences publiques, essais, débats, à
l'Institut canadien de Montréal, 1845-1871.* Montréal: Boréal, 1990.

————. *Louis-Antoine Dessaulles. Un seigneur libéral et anticlérical.*
Montréal: Fides.

Laski, Harold J. *Political Thought in England.* London: Oxford
University Press, 1948 (1920).

Le Devoir. *Le Québec et le lac Meech.* Montréal: Guérin, 1987.

Lequin, Yves. "La résistance des aristocraties." *Histoire économique et
sociale du monde*, tome 4. Pierre Léon, ed. Paris: Armand Collin,
1978.

Létourneau, Jocelyn. "L'imaginaire historique des jeunes Québécois."
Revue d'histoire de l'Amérique française 41:4 (1988): 553-575.

————, ed. *La question identitaire au Canada.* Québec: Presses de
l'Université Laval, 1994.

Levi, Margaret and Bates, Robert, eds. "The Political Economy of
French and English Development." *Politics and Society* 16
(septembre 1988): 2-3.

Lind, Michael. *The Next American Nation*. New York: Free Press, 1995.

Locke, John. *Two Treaties on Government*. New York: New American Library, 1960 (1690).

Lyotard, Jean-François. *La condition post-moderne*. Paris: Minuit, 1979.

Macpherson, C.B. *Burke*. Oxford: Oxford University Press, 1980.

———. *Principes et limites de la démocratie libérale*. Montréal: Boréal, 1985.

Macpherson, James. "Quebec Whistles Dixie." *Saturday Night* 113:2 (March 1998): 19-24.

Major, Robert. *Jean Rivard au l'art de réussir*. Québec: Presses de l'Université Laval, 1991.

Malinowski, Bronislaw. "Culture." *Encyclopaedia of the Social Sciences*. New York: NP, 1931.

Mann Trofimenkoff, Susan. *The Dream of Nation*. Toronto: Gage, 1983.

Mayer, Arno. *La persistance de l'Ancien Régime*. Paris: Flammarion, 1983.

McMillan, Alan D. *Native Peoples and Cultures of Canada*, Vancouver and Toronto: Douglas and McIntyre, 1995.

McRoberts, Kenneth. *Misconceiving Canada. The Struggle for National Unity*. Toronto: Oxford University Press, 1997.

——— and Dale Postgate. *Développement et modernisation du Québec*. Montréal: Boréal Express, 1983.

McRae, Kenneth. "The Structure of Canadian History." *The Founding of New Societies*. Louis Hartz, ed. New York: Harcourt, 1964.

Memmi, Albert. *Portrait du colonisé*. Montréal: L'étincelle, 1972.

Merton, Robert K. *Éléments de théorie et de méthode sociologique*. Paris: Plon, 1965.

Miner, Horace. *St-Denis: A French-Canadian Parish*. Chicago: Chicago University Press, 1939.

Moore, Barrington. *The Social Origins of Dictatorship and Democracy*. Boston: Beacon Press, 1966.

Morton, Desmond. *The New Democrats, 1961-1986: The Politics of Change*. Toronto: Copp Clark Pitman, 1986.

Nisbet, Robert. *La tradition sociologique*. Paris: Presses universitaires de France, 1984.

Nourry, Louis. *La pensée économique d'Étienne Parent: 1822-1852*. Thèse de maîtrise en histoire, Université de Montréal, 1969.

———. *La pensée politique d'Étienne Parent: 1831-1852*. Thèse de doctorat, Université de Montréal, 1971.

Ouellet, Fernand. "Étienne Parent et le mouvement du catholicisme social." *Bulletin des recherches historiques* 61, 3: 99.

Paquet, Gilles and Jean-Pierre Wallot. "Sur quelques discontinuités dans l'expérience socio-économique du Québec: une hypothèse." *RHAF* 35:4 (mars 1982): 483-522.

Parizeau, Gérard. "Mon ami Étienne Parent." *L'action universitaire*. II, 3 (février 1936): 50-51.

Peacock, Anthony A., ed. *Rethinking the Constitution*. Oxford: Oxford University Press, 1996.

Pellerin, Jean. *Le phénomène Trudeau*. Paris: Seghers, 1972.

Pocock, J. G. A. *The Machiavellian Moment*. Princeton: Princeton University Press, 1975.

Polanyi, Karl. *La grande transformation*. Paris: Gallimard, 1983.

Polin, Raymond. *La création des cultures.* Paris: Presses universitaires de France, 1993.

Radwanski, George. *Trudeau*. Toronto: Macmillan of Canada, 1978.

Rawls, John. *A Theory of Justice*. Cambridge: Harvard University Press, 1971.

———. Political Liberalism, New York: Columbia University Press, 1993.

Redfield, Robert. "The Folk Society." *American Journal of Sociology* LII,4 (1947): 29-308.

Rioux, Marcel. *La question du Québec*. Paris: Seghers, 1967.

———. "Sur l'évolution des idéologies au Québec." *Revue de l'Institut de sociologie* (1968): 112-118.

——— and Yves Martin. *La société canadienne-française*. Montréal: HMH, 1971.

Rocher, Guy. *Introduction à la sociologie générale*. Montréal: HMH, 1969.

Rorty, Richard. *Philosophy and the Mirror of Nature*. Oxford: Blackwell, 1980.

Rouillard, Jacques, ed. *Guide d'histoire du Québec*. Montréal: Méridien, 1991.

Rouillard, Jacques. *Les syndicats nationaux au Québec*. Québec: Presses de l'Université Laval, 1979.

Roy, Camille. *Manuel d'histoire de la littérature canadienne de langue française*. Montréal: Beauchemin, 1939.

————. *Morceaux choisis d'auteurs canadiens*. Montréal: Beauchemin, 1934.

Roy, Fernande. *Progrès, Harmonie, Liberté. Le libéralisme des milieux d'affaires francophones à Montréal au tournant du siècle*. Montréal: Boréal, 1988.

Rubinstein, W.D. "Wealth, elites and class structure in Britain." *Past and Present* 76 (1977).

Rudin, Ronald. *Banking en français. The French Banks of Quebec: 1835-1925*. Toronto: University of Toronto Press, 1985.

————. "La quête d'une société normale: critique de la réinterprétation de l'histoire du Québec." *Bulletin d'histoire politique* 3:2 (1994): 9-37.

————. "Revisionism and the Search for a Normal Society: A Critique of the Recent Québec Historical Writing." *Canadian Historical Review* 73 (1992): 60.

Said, Edward W., *Orientalism*, London, Routledge, 1978, 450 p.

————. *Culture and Imperialism*. New York: Pantheon Books, 1983.

Saint-Pierre, Arthur. "La littérature sociale canadienne-française avant la Confédération." *Mémoires de la société royale du Canada* (juin 1950): 67-94.

Sarup, Madan. *Post-Structuralism and Postmodernism*. Athens: University of Georgia Press, 1993 (1988).

Saul, John Ralston. *Reflections of a Siamese Twin: Canada at the End of the Twentieth Century*. Toronto: Viking, 1997.

Schull, Joseph. *Laurier* Montréal: MHM, 1968.

Shute, Stephen and Susan Hurley, eds. *On Human Rights: The Oxford Amnisty Lecture 1992*. New York: Basic Books, 1995.

Siedentop, Larry. "Liberalism: The Christian Connection." *Times Literary Supplement* 24-30 March 1989: 308.

Silver, A.I. *The French Canadian Idea of Confederation*. Toronto: University of Toronto Press, 1982.

Skocpol, Theda, ed. *Vision and Method in Historical Sociology*. Cambridge: Cambridge University Press, 1984.

————. *États et révolutions sociales*. Paris: Fayard, 1985.

Smith, Adam. *The Wealth of Nations*. Harmondsworth: Penguin Books, 1984 (1776).

Smith, Anthony D. *Theories of Nationalism*, New York: Holmes and Meier, 1983.

Stone, Laurence. "L'Angleterre de 1540 à 1880: pays de noblesse ouverte?" *Annales.Economie.Société.Civilisation* (jan-fév. 1985): 71-94.

Taylor, Charles. *Rapprocher les solitudes*. Québec: Presses de l'Université Laval, 1992.

———. *Philosophical Arguments*. Cambridge: Harvard University Press, 1995.

———. *Le malaise de la modernité*. Paris: Éditions du Cerf, 1994.

———. *Multiculturalisme*. Paris: Aubier, 1994.

Taylor, Charles. *Radical Tories*, Toronto: Anansi, 1982.

Thomas, David, ed. *Canada and the United States*. Peterborough: Broadview Press, 1993.

Tilly, Charles, ed. *The Formation of National States in Western Europe*. Princeton: Princeton University Press, 1975.

Tilly, Charles. *Big Structures, Large Processes, Huge Comparisons*. New York: Russel Foundation, 1984.

Tousignant, Pierre. "Problématique pour une nouvelle approche de la Constitution de 1791." *RHAF* 27:2 (septembre 1973): 181-234.

Tully, James. *Strange Multiplicity: Constitutionalism in an Age of Diversity*. Cambridge: Cambridge University Press, 1995.

Vachet, André. *L'idéologie libérale*. Paris: Anthropos, 1970.

Verley, Patrick. *La révolution industrielle: 1760-1870*. Paris: M A Éditions, 1985.

Vigod, Bernard L. *Quebec Before Duplessis: The Political Career of Louis-Alexandre Taschereau*. Montréal/Kingston: McGill-Queen's University Press, 1986.

Wade, Mason. *The French Canadians 1760-1967*. Vol. 1 1760-1910. Toronto: Macmillan of Canada, 1968.

———. *The French Canadians 1760-1967*. Vol. 2, 1911-1967. Toronto: Macmillan of Canada, 1983.

Wallot, Jean-Pierre. *Un Québec qui bougeait: Trame socio- politique du Québec au tournant du XIXe siècle*. Québec: Éditions du Boréal Express, 1973.

Waltzer, Michael. " Are There Limits to Liberalism?" *New York Review of Books* 19 October 1995.

Weber, Max. *L'éthique protestante et l'esprit du capitalisme*. Paris: Plon, 1964.

Whitaker, Reg. *A Sovereign Idea*. Montréal and Kingston: McGill-Queen's University Press, 1992.

Williams, Raymond. *The Country and the City*. New York: Oxford University Press, 1973.

———. *Cobbett*. Oxford: Oxford University Press, 1983.

Williamson, Jeffrey G. "Why Was British Growth So Slow During the Industrial Revolution?" *The Journal of Economic History* 44, 3 (September 1984): 687-689.

"We the People of Québec." *Globe and Mail* September 1995: 1.

Wilson-Smith, Anthony. "The Bouchard File." *Maclean's* 110:35, (September 1997): 12-17.

Wood, Neal. *John Locke and Agragarian Capitalism*. Berkeley: University of California Press, 1984.

Woronoff, Denis. "La révolution a-t-elle été une catastrophe économique? " *L'histoire* 113 (juillet-août 1998): 110-116.